THE BIRTH OF
KIRTAN

THE BIRTH OF
KIRTAN

The Life & Teachings of Chaitanya

Ranchor Prime

PROLOGUE BY JAI UTTAL
FOREWORD BY SHIVA REA
PREFACE BY RADHANATH SWAMI

MANDALA
PUBLISHING

San Rafael, California

MANDALA
PUBLISHING

PO Box 3088
San Rafael, CA 94912
www.mandalapublishing.com

Text copyright © 2012 by Ranchor Prime
Prologue copyright © 2012 by Jai Uttal
Foreword copyright © 2012 by Shiva Rea
Preface copyright © 2012 by Radhanath Swami
Illustrations copyright © 2012 Mandala Publishing

Retold from the sixteenth-century Bengali sources:
Sri Chaitanya Charitamrita by Krishnadas Kaviraj Goswami
(translated by His Divine Grace A. C. Bhaktivedanta Swami
Prabhupada) and *Sri Chaitanya Bhagavat* by Vrindavana Das
Thakur (translated by Kusakratha das)

Library of Congress Cataloging-in-Publication Data available.

ISBN: 978-1-60887-107-0

Visit the author at:
mandala-earthaware.blogspot.com/p/Birth-of-Kirtan.html

Insight Editions, in association with Roots of
Peace, will plant two trees for each tree used
in the manufacturing of this book. Roots of Peace is an internationally
renowned humanitarian organization dedicated to eradicating land mines
worldwide and converting war-torn lands into productive farms and
wildlife habitats. Together, we will plant two million fruit and nut trees
in Afghanistan and provide farmers there with the skills and support
necessary for sustainable land use.

10 9 8 7 6 5 4 3 2 1

Manufactured in China

Pages ii–iii: *Chaitanya leads* kirtan, *public singing of names of God, in the
streets of sixteenth-century Navadvipa. These ecstatic* kirtan *processions were the
essence of Chaitanya's practice and teachings and transformed the consciousness of
the community.*

DEDICATION

·····

to my guru, who introduced me to Sri Chaitanya

to my friend Ramdas

and to all who have ever shed a tear for God

Contents

BOOK THREE
Traveling & Teaching

BOOK FOUR
The Ocean of Love

PROLOGUE
by Jai Uttal

....

Beware! This book is dangerous. The very pages are on fire with a divine passion. The words burn with the fervor of incendiary love. If you cherish the path of a moderate life, please find something else to read. But if you're ready to be ignited by the flame of Radharani's longing for her beloved, read on . . .

This is an amazingly wonderful text. Not because of the words in it, although Ranchor's writing is never less than beautiful, but because of the living presence that breathes, sings, weeps, laughs, and dances through every page. Call him a saint; call him a guru; call him an avatar. It matters not. The echoes of Sri Krishna Chaitanya's footsteps are still shaking this world to its core. The distant melody of his *kirtan* is still awakening hearts across all the universes, known and unknown.

May we, for just one moment of our lives, experience the divine earthshaking love that Mahaprabhu gave away so freely. May we chant God's names as if our very lives depended on it. May we be blessed with the grace to serve one who serves the servants of the great ones. Let us bow to the Lotus Feet of the Golden Avatar. I bow to this holy book for inspiring me, once again, on the endless path of love.

In closing, I must lodge a rather serious complaint against this biography, which has destroyed the calmness of my heart. It is way too short! Why must the reader be drawn into the divine world of Mahaprabhu only to be cast out again after a mere 216 pages? What injustice! What cruel agony! Well, perhaps there will be a sequel . . . Many sequels . . . The life of Nityananda . . . Gadadhar . . . And all the blessed companions of Radha and her beloved Govinda when they appeared on the Earth five hundred years ago . . .

Hari bol!

Left: *Chaitanya captured the hearts of the people of Bengal with his fervent chanting and ecstatic dancing, calling upon his beloved Krishna.*

FOREWORD
by Shiva Rea

·········

The life of Sri Chaitanya has reverberated for over five hundred years as an extraordinary teaching of fearless devotion—a story for all of humanity and one that many Western yoga practitioners have yet to know. It reminds us that challenges and forces of oppression can be overcome with the power of sublime love and grace.

It is hard for us to imagine the local forces breaking down the doors of our home to stop us from singing *kirtan* and dancing, or breaking drums, or even using brutality to oppress the forces of love. But this was the ground from which Sri Chaitanya Mahaprabhu offered his first public *kirtan* in Bengal in 1510.

At the time of Sri Chaitanya's life, there was a strong division of caste, men, and women—a ritual hierarchy that controlled one's direct experience of the Source. Although Sri Chaitanya came from a learned family, his love of Krishna filled his private practice with *sankirtan:* chanting and dancing for the divine.

The people of Mayapur were so inspired by the ecstatic chanting of Sri Chaitanya that they could hear emanating from his home, they started to echo the chanting of the divine name of Krishna. This tide of unity brought on the brutal oppression of the local Kazi, the Muslim ruler of Mayapur, who, at the encouragement of the Hindu religious elite, tried to stop this rise of love through fear and violence.

Sri Chaitanya's response is a guiding light for all beings. For the first time, he brought his practice to the street. He asked all of the local people to come together to light a torch and make a procession to the local Kazi's residence, singing and dancing with the *kirtan*. Choosing love over fear, the procession swelled, as tens of thousands of people took the streets, following Sri Chaitanya and his beloved disciples to the house of the Kazi.

What happened that night, on the first public *kirtan*, is one of the many stories of Sri Chaitanya's life that all beings on this planet will be inspired and

Left: *Nityananda worked tirelessly to spread Chaitanya's practice of* kirtan *in love for Krishna.*

blessed to know. At the darkest hour, Sri Chaitanya brought forth a blazing love, transforming fear and violence through the vibration of mantra. He initiated the Bhakti movement with a literal "movement" of devotional dance, enabling men and women from all castes to move together, united by the source of love.

This summer at the annual gathering of Bhakti Fest in Joshua Tree, which brought thousands of people together from all backgrounds and forms of yoga for four days of continuous *kirtan*, I was moved to tears as Radhanath Swamiji retold this story to me from the core backstage, as Jai Uttal and band were getting ready for the next *kirtan*. While I also had been telling this story to my student friends for years, there were many details that I had not known that brought subtler layers of teaching to light.

I have been looking for an accessible and in-depth resource to bring into my own life, as well as to share with friends on the path, and now have in this precious book, which has come at a time when the courage to rise in love over fear is once again gaining momentum around the world.

May we remember the power of love within us that is transforming us all. May we chant, dance, sing, meditate, and study in freedom, in remembrance of Sri Chaitanya's incredible life and legacy, knowing that there are still many people in the world who do not have access to this sacred flow. I am grateful to Ranchor Prime and Mandala Publishing for making this book available for us all right now, to Radhanath Swami for being a living example of Sri Chaitanya, and to the amazing *bhaktas* around the world who are living this love. May the love of Krishna and Radha be accessible to all in the form of continuing *kirtan* and teachings of the great Vaishnava lineage from Sri Chaitanya.

Sri Sri Chaitanya Mahaprabhu ki jai!
Radhe Shyam!

Right: *Throughout his life, Chaitanya shared continuous kirtan with his companions and devotees.*

সার্ব ভৌমে দেখাইল প্রভু, বিভিন্ন রূপ।
পাছে শ্যাম, পাশে বিষ্ণু, স্বকীয় স্বরূপ॥

PREFACE
by Radhanath Swami

....

s the rising full moon spreads its golden rays, dispelling darkness and giving pleasure to all, Chaitanya, the Golden Avatara, appeared in the world to bestow infinite light, hope, and love.

Stories of Chaitanya's life and mission irresistibly attracted me when I first encountered them as a young man. My heart thirsted for more. I was spellbound by the infinite love and compassion that he expressed in such extraordinary ways. Yet he was simple, humble, and accessible to everyone. Ranchor Prime has offered a great blessing to humanity in giving us *The Birth of Kirtan: The Life & Teachings of Chaitanya*. It is an intimate glimpse into the incredible biography of the Golden Avatara.

Avatara is the word used in the ancient Sanskrit texts to denote the Supreme Lord, who descends into the material world to extend compassion upon all beings. The Sanskrit texts in which it appeared predicted Chaitanya's appearance thousands of years prior to his descent five hundred years ago in the form of a beautiful human being with a golden complexion. His original, divine identity remained hidden so that he could teach devotion to the general public by playing the role of a devotee.

He ignited a spiritual revolution. Chaitanya defied the superficial, oppressive, and sectarian boundaries of his times by declaring that pure, ecstatic love for Krishna (God as the all-attractive Person) is the privilege of all souls regardless of their caste or station in life. He taught and exemplified how this love inspires compassion for all beings. He proclaimed that the precious treasure of ecstatic love is within our hearts and that everyone is entitled to it. He distributed love of God through the simple process of *kirtan*: the chanting of the holy names. God has many names, he taught, and each of them is empowered to awaken the dormant love within our hearts.

He fearlessly confronted the prejudice of the oppressive caste system by establishing an untouchable, Haridas, as the highest guru for chanting the

Left: *Chaitanya shared his divine identity as an avatar of Krishna with only a few intimate companions.*

holy names. He exposed the ego of materialistic religionists by accepting a humble gift of leaves from a poverty-stricken banana leaf seller, Shridhar, as the ultimate offering to the Lord. He taught that it is sincere, loving intent that is all-important, not the material value of a thing.

In his time, people who dared to practice such beliefs were beaten, exploited, or killed by the military. A tyrant, Chand Kazi, ruled the government and innocent people lived in constant fear. It was Chaitanya who began a nonviolent civil disobedience movement in defiance of the Kazi's oppressive rule, setting a precedent that would be taken up 430 years later by Mahatma Gandhi. Chaitanya led a procession of hundreds of thousands of protesters all chanting God's names through the town and to the door of the Kazi's home. The combination of Chaitanya's power, humility, and kindness transformed Chand Kazi's heart, and from then on he honored all faiths with affection.

The Lord restored life to a dead child; transformed murderers, robbers, and drunkards into humble saints; and infused love of God into tigers, deer, and elephants, inducing them to dance in ecstasy. His own magnificent dancing was an outpouring of his ecstatic love for Krishna, and it flooded the hearts of an entire population with that love. He was the transcendent Lord, the embodiment of supreme bliss, who could not bear to see the sufferings of his children.

Chaitanya extended his mercy equally to kings and stray dogs, housewives and ascetics, scholars and farmers, millionaires and beggars. The only qualification was to open their hearts to accept his grace. Yet in his early life, he played the part of an ordinary child devoted to his mother, Sachi, and was tied to her by filial affection. Who can understand the lives of saints, yogis, avatars, and other emissaries of love for God? Their behavior follows no familiar patterns. Their ecstasies confuse all who are unfamiliar with such depths of emotion. They defy conventions and challenge both religious and secular codes of conduct. They are not of this world. Yet seeing into their lives can inspire us to awaken the love they embody.

Ranchor Prime has provided a valuable service by combining stories of Chaitanya's life with the sensitivity and care that come from the author's lifetime of Krishna devotion. This heartfelt rendering of the two primary biographies of Chaitanya is destined to become a classic of mystic devotional writing.

Chaitanya (center) organized nonviolent public rallies that inspired Gandhi's movement of the 1930s.

INTRODUCTION

········

Sri Krishna Chaitanya was that rare individual: a person whose life embodied his message. He wrote no books, organized no mission, had few direct disciples, and only lived to be forty-eight. During his adult years, he was fully detached from the world, and virtually his only form of public teaching was *kirtan*, singing the names of God. In his final years, he withdrew into seclusion from all but his closest companions. Yet in his brief time on earth, he sowed the seeds of a spiritual movement that even now unfolds across the world.

The message of Chaitanya was simple: look for the company of those devoted to the service of God and together hear about God and chant God's names. By so doing, your love will grow and you will find lasting happiness. He gave profound revelations of the highest reality to a handful of intimate disciples, who preserved them for posterity in Sanskrit and Bengali poetry inscribed on palm leaves or the bark of trees. Until the dawn of the twentieth century, he and his teachings were unknown outside India. It was, however, foretold that one day he would be known everywhere. In these urgent times of planetary renewal and transformation, this prophecy is coming to pass and his story can at last be told to the world.

Golden Moon

Chaitanya was born in Navadvip, West Bengal, in the year 1486 and mysteriously disappeared in 1533. He spent his last years in Puri, the then capital city of Orissa in Eastern India. He taught the path of devotion, known in Sanskrit as bhakti yoga, and shared his love for Krishna with tens of thousands across India. During his lifetime, he was known as Gaurachandra (golden moon), Nimai (having been born under a *neem* tree), Vishvambhar (sustainer of the world), Krishna Chaitanya (living spirit of Krishna), and Mahaprabhu (great master).

From an early age, he showed miraculous powers that persuaded many

Left: *Chaitanya, in later life, spent his time in the company
of friends, absorbed in hearing of the sweetness and loving
pastimes of Radha and Krishna.*

who were close to him that he was a divine avatar, a manifestation of the Supreme. Although in public he always denied this, his followers believed him to be an incarnation of Krishna.

The Mystery of Chaitanya

Chaitanya was a paradox. Tradition tells us that he revealed his divine identity to a few favored devotees, yet on each occasion he swore them to secrecy. He showed the utmost humility and lived a simple life, yet he was also one of the most exuberant religious figures of medieval India. He urged his followers not to try to see God, rather to feel the absence of God in this earthly realm and embrace such feelings of divine separation.[1] Yet he longed to see Krishna so intensely that he spoke of little else.

Chaitanya lived in a perpetual state of divine longing. His powerful emotions often swept him into ecstatic states. We are told he possessed extraordinary charisma and physical beauty, which overwhelmed all who met him. He was said to have been seven feet tall, broad-shouldered and long-armed, with dark flowing hair and huge lotus-shaped eyes. His complexion was described as *gaura*, golden, and he often manifested a shining effulgence. He was quick-witted, was blessed with a penetrating deep voice, and was a powerful scholar and orator. It was small wonder that he made an indelible impression wherever he went.

For Chaitanya, God was far away, hidden from his creation, yet as near as a heartbeat. Chaitanya's mood of longing, of separation from the divine beloved, was expressed in the love felt for Krishna by the *gopis*, the cowherd girls of the forest of Vrindavan. Stories of Krishna tell us how, in their youth, Krishna and the *gopis* had intense loving affairs; during the day they played in the forest and at night they danced under the moonlight, inspiring images that have been immortalized in some of India's most memorable art, music, drama, and literature. After Krishna left Vrindavan, he and the *gopis* spent the rest of their lives apart, always remembering the love they once shared. This constant remembrance between lover and beloved was epitomized in the love between Krishna and the *gopi* Radha, a metaphor for the intense longing between the soul and God. This was the theme that dominated Chaitanya's life.

His famous biographer, Krishnadas Kaviraj, based his work on the journals kept by Chaitanya's closest companions. His epic biographical poem *Sri Chaitanya Charitamrita* (1615) was completed in his old age, and is one of the masterpieces of medieval Bengali literature. The poet poured a lifetime of devotion and learning into his work, capturing the mystical spirit of Chaitanya's life and teachings.

Krishnadas opened his work by explaining the identity and significance of Sri Chaitanya. The following pages summarize the poet's prologue.

The Vaishnava Faith

The ancient Vaishnava faith, which existed prior to Chaitanya, taught that God, Vishnu, is the supreme maintainer of all life. Vishnu exists as Brahman, the all-pervading spirit that is at the basis of all existence; as Paramatma, the Inner Guide who lives in the hearts of all beings; and as Bhagavan, the Original Supreme Person, who is love personified and the source of all that is. These three aspects of God—as pure energy, as guiding presence in the hearts of all, and as the personification of love—coexist eternally.

God appears to earthly vision in many forms, like waves of the ocean, and these forms illuminate the world like candles in the darkness. The one original candle, source of the many, is Krishna, the Supreme Personality of Godhead. Chaitanya devoted his life to Krishna. This original Krishna, said the poet Krishnadas, entered the world as Sri Chaitanya. The intentions for his incarnation were three.

Krishna's Incarnation as Chaitanya

Wherever Chaitanya went, he taught people to come together and sing Krishna's names. This simple practice, called *kirtan*, was so powerful and profound that it could banish illusion and uncover the soul's natural love for God. Chaitanya's favorite practice was *sankirtan*, community *kirtan*, shared often with great gatherings of devoted chanters. The mission to teach and share *kirtan* was the first intention for Chaitanya's incarnation.

A second intention was revealed in Chaitanya's mood of intense spiritual love. Krishna radiates pure love that flows perpetually between him and his eternal companion Radha. Their love extends to fill all creation. She is the personification of pure love for Krishna, who is never separated from her beloved. To share their love with all beings, these two united as one person in the divine form of Chaitanya. This, wrote Krishnadas, was the second intention for his incarnation.

The third and secret intention for Chaitanya's incarnation was to fulfill Krishna's intense desire to become Radha. As the manifestation of purest love, the Goddess Radha enchants Krishna and her spirit inspires the whole creation. Longing to experience love from Radha's unique perspective, Krishna chose to "become" her, to become a devotee who loves Krishna more than life itself. To accomplish this, Krishna, by appearing as Chaitanya, wanted to experience the spirit of Radha in three distinct ways: to taste the joy of her love; to see his own beauty as only she could; and to feel her ecstasy in being loved by him. To appreciate these inner reasons for Krishna's incarnation in the form of Chaitanya is possible with the blessings of Chaitanya's intimate companions, wrote the poet Krishnadas.

Nityananda, the "Brother" of Chaitanya

Chief among these companions was Chaitanya's friend Nityananda, who was born in East Bengal around 1474. He was as a brother to Chaitanya[2] and led his movement in Bengal. These two, Gaura and Nitai, wrote the poet Krishnadas, were like the sun and moon rising together to light up the darkness of the world. They lit up the outer world and illuminated the hearts of their devotees, dissolving their shadows and awakening them to love for God. Chaitanya was the incarnation of Krishna, and Nityananda was the incarnation of Balaram.

In the eternal world of the spirit, as revealed to the faithful readers of the *Srimad Bhagavatam*, the ancient Sanskrit scripture encoding the life of Krishna, Balaram is Krishna's brother, and he loves to serve Krishna in numerous ways. While Krishna plays with his friends, for instance, Balaram expands as Vishnu to create the material worlds. First he creates and then enters countless universes of matter, supporting them in a multitude of forms. Vishnu is present throughout creation, yet he is also the seed from which all creation flows, and he enters the hearts of all beings as the Inner Guide who cares for the world. As the one who cares for the world and all within it, Balaram, or Rama, is pure unconditional love and the original guru of all.

Nityananda, wrote the poet Krishnadas, was a personification of Balaram, reaching out to souls lost in this created world of birth and death, and calling them back to Krishna.

Advaita, Who Prepared the Way

Advaita[3] was born in Bengal in 1434, fifty-two years before Chaitanya. The poet identified him as an incarnation of Vishnu, creator of the world, yet like Chaitanya, Advaita saw himself as one who served others. He shared with Nityananda the mood of being a servant of Chaitanya. The joy of service, wrote the poet, is a thousand times greater than the joy of merging into God. Service was the mood of whoever loved Krishna—as elder, friend, or lover—and brought unlimited joy.

"I am a servant of Sri Chaitanya and a servant of his servants," sang Advaita. This joyful song of service was the song of all creation. Those who aspired to pure oneness with God missed the ecstasy of loving service. Even Krishna wanted to feel the emotion of loving service, so he descended in the form of Chaitanya.

Oneness in Diversity

The poet Krishnadas wrote that Krishna appeared in this world as Chaitanya, bringing with him Nityananda, Advaita, and a host of companions to act alongside him in his human drama. These companions were born across Bengal and Orissa, to assemble in Navadvip ready for the appearance of Krishna. Among them were Gadadhar,[4] who became Chaitanya's lifelong friend and confidante, and Srivas,[5] whose simple wisdom and love inspired Chaitanya and his followers.

Chaitanya's message was embodied in these five persons united in a single love. Krishnadas called them the Pancha Tattva, the five truths: Chaitanya, Nityananda, Advaita, Gadadhar, and Srivas. These five danced, sang, laughed and cried, sending forth waves of love that transformed Hindu society in Eastern India in the early sixteenth century.

Devotees of Chaitanya invoked the divine presence of the fivefold Pancha Tattva by singing their names at the start of *kirtan* using this famous Sanskrit mantra:

sri krishna chaitanya prabhu nityananda
sri advaita gadadhara srivas adi gaura bhakta vrinda

In Chaitanya's day, India was alive with philosophical debate. The Sanskrit literatures, particularly the *Vedanta Sutra*, *Upanishads*, and *Bhagavad Gita*, were the source books for exploration and dispute about nature, the soul, and God.

Chaitanya was no stranger to philosophy and in his youth was a brilliant debater. His ecstatic religion of Krishna Consciousness was built on foundations of philosophy and common sense. His teachings emerged in a series of encounters with learned teachers during his travels around India, and were later recorded for posterity by his direct disciples, to be passed down through generations of teachers.

The essence of his philosophy was known as *Achintya-bhedabheda*, that is, "inconceivable oneness and difference." This is the term he used to describe the relationship between God and the living beings. While some teachers proclaimed oneness, and others proclaimed duality, Chaitanya taught a balanced view: the living beings and God are one *and* different simultaneously. He explained this by saying that we are one with God in quality but not in quantity. The soul is like a drop of water compared to an ocean. In essence the drop of water and the ocean are one, but the ocean is always greater than the drop.

Some speak of God as Creator, some as Soul of the World, some as Inner Guide; some as Vishnu, some as Rama, some as Shiva; some as the Goddess, the creative force of life; some as the Holy Trinity, some as Allah and some as Jehovah. God or Goddess are shown to each of us according to our capacity to receive and to our inspiration. All these divine visions are reflected in the inspiration and wisdom channeled through Chaitanya to his followers.

The Chain of Devotion

The story of Chaitanya and his teachings was carried on a wave of love all the way down to the present day. It passed through the hearts of innumerable devotees, transmitted through an unbroken chain of teachers.

Five centuries after Chaitanya's appearance, the chain of devotion and wisdom was brought to the West by Chaitanya's devotee, Bhaktivedanta Swami, Srila Prabhupada. In 1969, he established near the British Museum in London a beautiful temple dedicated to Radha and Krishna.

In that temple, when I was a young art student, I heard Prabhupada's message delivered through his disciples, and later I met Prabhupada and was initiated as his disciple. So, I too became a follower of Chaitanya.

I cannot tell the story of Chaitanya as one might a standard history or biography. It is a mystical and mysterious tale, recorded by his contemporaries and set into sublime poetry. The two sixteenth-century Bengali poets and philosophers, Vrindavan Das Thakur and Krishnadas Kaviraj Goswami, have been my guides in finding the authentic story of Chaitanya, and this book is based on their accounts. Through my guru, I was blessed with the opportunity to tell this story, which he published in the 1970s in a translation that filled many volumes laden with devotion and poetic wisdom. I am here to pass on this amazing story in simple language to a new audience.

Our world is going through momentous changes; hearts and minds are open as never before to receive fresh inspiration. I am a messenger. Please be patient with my limitations, for this is a magical story. Chaitanya is not of this world, although he undoubtedly lived and breathed here. His life belongs on another plane of reality. Just to hear his story with an open mind and heart will heal your soul and draw you to his eternal realm of love.

The poet Krishnadas Kaviraj (1520–1617) composed his biography of Chaitanya in the twilight years of his life: Sri Chaitanya Charitamrita *is a masterpiece of Bengali literature.*

Following pages: *Vishvambhar, preparing to leave Bengal, was initiated as a* sannyasi *and renamed Sri Krishna Chaitanya; all who witnessed the ceremony wept with sorrow and love.*

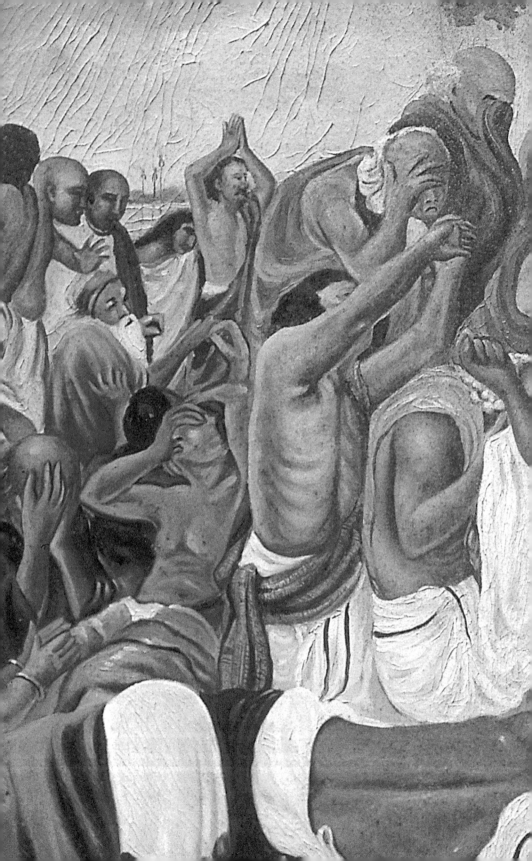

BOOK ONE

Childhood

Moonrise

In the spring of 1486, as the full moon rose into a total eclipse over Bengal, a beautiful boy was born.

The way had been prepared by Advaita. He was called Acharya, which means "teacher." He saw the confused condition of the world and prayed for divine help. In answer to Advaita's prayers, Krishna descended from the spiritual world and was born in Navadvip. So the poets tell us.

Advaita Acharya lived in fifteenth-century Bengal in the village of Shantipur. The fields around his village were flat and fertile, watered by the Ganges and her tributaries in the populous land of Nadia. The district was dominated by Navadvip, on the bank of the Ganges, 150 miles inland from the Bay of Bengal. This was a prosperous and cultured town, famous as a center of learning. All day, teachers gathered beside bathing areas, called *ghats*, that lined the River Ganges. There they taught their students the intricacies of logic and Sanskrit grammar. By evening, the town came alive with celebrations in honor of the Goddess.

Advaita Acharya had a town house in Navadvip, where he was the senior teacher of his community. In his main home in the village of Shantipur, he organized regular prayer meetings for local Vaishnavas, whose tradition was in decline. Advaita saw around him a society preoccupied with material pleasures: people were losing interest in the Vaishnava faith.

Vaishnavism upheld an ordered life centered around the worship of Vishnu, maintainer of the worlds. This was being replaced in Navadvip by ritual worship of the Goddess in pursuit of worldly happiness.[6] Advaita believed that material enjoyment would not satisfy the inner longing of the soul, whereas devotion to Vishnu would bring people true peace and happiness. On his own, he felt powerless to change society. Every day he prayed to Krishna, the loving and personal form of Vishnu, to descend among the people and teach love for God.

Advaita was friendly with a gentle *brahmana* named Jagannath Mishra, who had moved from Eastern Bengal to settle in Navadvip. Mishra's wife, Sachi, bore eight daughters, but each of them died soon after birth. Still, throughout her prolonged struggle to bear children, she never lost faith in God, continually praying with her husband for at least one healthy child. At last their prayers were answered when their ninth child was born a strong and healthy boy, whom they named Vishvarup. His arrival filled them with happiness.

Soon after, Sachi conceived again. This time she felt the spirit of God descend upon her, and in her joy she radiated spiritual beauty. After their succession of misfortunes, it seemed now, with one strong child and a second one on the way, their sorrows had finally come to an end.

Friends stopped Jagannath on the street to congratulate him and to offer him gifts. In Sachi's dreams, she saw angels singing prayers to the child in her womb. Both of them felt sure that a special child was about to be born.

That evening the moon entered a full eclipse and a smoky twilight enveloped the world. During this time of shadows, people feared the influence of the lunar eclipse, believing it brought misfortune. To counteract this they sought the all-embracing shelter of Mother Ganges, immersing themselves in her sacred waters and offering prayers. Even those who were not normally observant took these precautions, and with one voice the people chanted the names of God. At this time, with the world prophetically resounding to Krishna's names, Sachi's son was born.

Advaita saw the eclipse and knew in his heart that a special event was taking place. He bathed in the Ganges and chanted with great joy. The Vaishnavas who saw him realized that he was seeing something more than just a lunar eclipse. Though they didn't fully understand, they joined him in his chanting.

Everywhere the atmosphere grew calm and people's minds were filled with peace. Musicians sang and played musical instruments; people danced in the streets; some even saw celestial beings in the sky and heard their music wafting through the heavens.

As soon as his son was born, Jagannath Mishra called his family priests to chant celebratory prayers. Crowds of well-wishers brought gifts to honor Sachi and her newborn child. Chief among them was Sita, the wife of Advaita Acharya, who came from Shantipur bringing bracelets, necklaces, silks, sandalwood, and gold coins to present to this special child. She believed he had come in answer to her husband's prayers.

Protector of the World

A regular stream of friends and relatives visited mother and child. They noticed a surprising thing: when the child cried, the chanting of Krishna's names would pacify him, causing him to smile. The instant they stopped singing, however, he again started to cry. They soon realized that he wanted them to sing God's names, and this they gladly did, clapping their hands and filling the air with the sound of "Hari, Hari!" As they chanted, the women saw that the child shone with a golden light. So they named him Gaurahari, Golden Lord.

Strange things happened around the house. Visitors saw ethereal presences in the shadows or peering through the windows. Some said these were demigods who had come to honor the divine child; others feared they were evil spirits. Uncertain what was happening, people guarded the house with their prayers and sang Krishna's names all the more.

When it was time for the child's name-giving ceremony, Sachi's father, Nilambara Chakravarti, calculated his grandson's horoscope.

"This child has deep intelligence and will become a great scholar," pronounced Nilambara. "He will be a ruler of unimaginable glory. Perhaps he is the *brahmana*, long foretold by our people, who is to become the savior of Bengal."

The horoscope predicted that the child would teach the path of truth, bringing good fortune to everyone around him. Because it appeared that he would bless the whole world, Nilambara gave him the name Vishvambhar, meaning "Protector of the World." And since he was born under a *neem* tree, which had the reputation of driving away harmful spirits and whose leaves had healing properties, his mother called him Nimai. This became his childhood name among his family and friends.

After the name-giving came the traditional choosing of gifts by the infant, intended to reveal his calling in life. Three offerings were spread before baby Nimai: a tantalizing plate of sweets and puffed rice, a glittering mound of coins, and the holy book *Srimad Bhagavatam* laid on a cloth. Guests gathered around to see which gift he would choose. To everyone's delight, he took hold of the *Bhagavatam* with great enthusiasm. The ladies present sang Krishna's names in joy, and as they did so, little Nimai danced on their laps.

The beautiful child began to crawl around the house. About his waist was a belt with tiny bells, which tinkled as he moved.

One day, as he played in the courtyard, a large cobra emerged from the bushes and coiled itself around him. Nimai wasn't afraid. He played with the serpent and lay back among its coils, gurgling with delight. His mother came into the courtyard and saw what was happening. She cried in alarm and rushed forward, at which the snake uncoiled itself and glided harmlessly away. Nimai wanted to crawl after it and catch it, but he was scooped up and carried to safety, while the snake disappeared and was not seen again. Everyone believed he had been rescued from certain death.

Soon Nimai started to walk. Mischievous and full of curiosity, he entered neighbors' houses and crept into their kitchens, where he ate their food and drank their milk. Sometimes in childish frustration he broke their clay pots. However, when the women caught him, they were so charmed by him that they laughed and let him go.[7]

His mother and father were enchanted by their beautiful child. They felt certain he was no ordinary mortal, but a divine being. His shining face was bordered by curling locks, his eyes were large like the petals of a lotus flower, and his smile was captivating. When they saw Nimai, people spontaneously offered him gifts such as bananas or ornaments—even those meeting him for the first time. He cleverly used these gifts as bribes to make everyone sing Krishna's names. This game went on until all his family and their friends were chanting the names of God. When they did so, he would laugh and dance, and when they did not, he would weep. So all came under his influence.

One day, Nimai, decorated with jeweled ornaments, was playing outside his home. Absorbed in his play, he wandered off in the direction of the Ganges, where his parents couldn't see him. Just then, two thieves approached and observed his shining ornaments. They could not believe their luck.

"This beautiful child is a treasure trove," one said. "Let us kidnap him and steal his jewels." So saying, they enticed Nimai with sweets.

"Little boy, you look lost," they said. "Come with us and we will carry you home." One of them lifted Nimai onto his shoulders.

"Yes, " laughed Nimai playfully, "Please take me home."

Nimai enjoyed riding on their shoulders, but at home his absence had been noticed, and all were frantically calling his name and searching for him.

The thieves continued their journey with Nimai on their shoulders, moving quickly until they thought they were a safe distance from his home. They set him down and were about to strip him of his jewels, when they realized they had run in a circle and arrived right back in front of Nimai's house. Jagannath saw them and came running. He gratefully picked up his little boy, and was about to thank the two strangers, but they fled in panic.

Everyone wanted to know where Nimai had been and what had happened to him. But he spoke kindly of the two men who "gave him a ride" on their shoulders.

"I wanted to go to the Ganges, father, but I got lost," he said sweetly. "Then those two men picked me up and brought me home." Jagannath again wanted to thank the men, but they were never seen again.

Divine Footprints

Little Nimai ran about the house, delighting his parents as they watched their son's energetic explorations. One day, Jagannath, sitting down to study his books, called his son: "Nimai, please bring me the *Bhagavatam*," he asked.

Nimai scampered over to where the sacred book was kept and struggled to lift it in his little arms. Watching his obedient son staggering toward him with the weighty volume, Jagannath distinctly heard the tinkling of ankle bells, as if coming from Nimai. Sachi heard the sound too and looked around with curiosity. Nimai wore no ankle bells that either of them could see. Yet they both clearly heard this musical sound.

Later that day they witnessed another curious sign. Nimai had gone out to play and Sachi was busy cleaning. She was about to sweep the floor when she noticed small footprints everywhere. These were no ordinary prints, for they showed the unmistakable marks of Krishna's feet. The soles of Krishna's feet were renowned for bearing the marks of a flag, a thunderbolt, a fish, and a lotus flower. She saw these footprints all over their floor, but could not bring herself to believe that her son had made them. She called Jagannath and together they wondered how these divine footprints could have appeared. The only explanation they could think of was that their Vishnu deity, whom they prayed to daily, had come to life and blessed their house with his footprints. Excitedly, they called Nimai to show him the wonder.

"Vishnu himself must have descended from our household shrine and secretly walked around our home to bless us," said Sachi, "And as he walked his ankle bells tinkled."

Nimai looked at the footprints he had left in the dust and simply smiled.

··•••••·

ONE DAY A PILGRIM ENTERED NAVADVIP on his way through Bengal. He was a retired *brahmana* who had dedicated himself to visiting all the holy places of India. Around his neck he carried a small deity of Bala Gopal, baby Krishna, whom he worshipped. The *brahmana* no longer had a home, but felt at peace wherever he was, confident in the Lord's protection, and looked after by the kindness of people he met on the road. Jagannath Mishra met the pilgrim in the marketplace and invited him to stay in his house.

"It would be an honor for us if you would cook for Krishna in our house," suggested Jagannath.

The pilgrim agreed to this invitation, and Jagannath brought him to his house. There he gave him a place for worship and thoroughly cleaned the kitchen, providing his guest with grains, fresh vegetables, milk, and ghee with which to cook. When midday arrived, a beautifully prepared meal was ready and the pilgrim began to offer it to Bala Gopal.

The pilgrim placed his offering before his deity of baby Krishna and sat down to recite prayers, calling Krishna to come and eat. As soon as he started chanting the mantras, Nimai entered the room and, as if in answer to the pilgrim's call, began to help himself to the food on the altar.

"Stop! You have spoiled my offering," cried the pilgrim, "for now the food cannot be offered to Krishna."

Jagannath heard his cry and hurried into the room. He saw his mischievous son eating and chased him away.

"Do not be angry with the child," implored the pilgrim. "Bring me whatever ingredients you have left and I will cook again."

Jagannath was pacified and took the boy to a neighbor's house where he was carefully watched. Meanwhile, the pilgrim cooked for a second time and by late afternoon he was ready to make another offering. As he began to chant his prayers, Nimai somehow escaped from the watchful eyes of the women next door and appeared as before, smiling and eating with great satisfaction. The pilgrim called out loudly: "Help! This boy has come again to spoil my offering." This time he was upset and said to Jagannath, "Krishna does not want my offering today."

Jagannath was mortified that this misfortune should befall the pilgrim for a second time when he was an honored guest in his house, and he threatened to punish Nimai.

"What good will your punishment do?" admonished the pilgrim. "He is only a child and should not be blamed. I must accept Krishna's will: today I fast."

Just then Nimai's older brother, Vishvarup, arrived home from school and was amused to learn of his little brother's pranks.

Vishvarup's presence calmed everyone, as it always did, and soon he had convinced the pilgrim to cook a third time. More provisions were brought and Nimai was taken away yet again. This time he was brought to another room with his mother and put to bed. Soon he fell asleep and all was quiet.

With daylight fading, the pilgrim settled down to cook for a third time. As night fell, the adults felt sleepy and all of them went to bed. Alone in the flickering light of a lamp, the pilgrim prepared to make his offering. He slipped into a deep meditation, contemplating the form of his beloved Bala Gopal and making heartfelt prayers for Krishna to accept his offering.

In the darkness, Nimai stirred. Soundlessly, he slipped from the bedroom and came in answer to the pilgrim's prayers. The pilgrim opened his eyes but did not see Nimai. Instead, he saw before him the very same Krishna of his meditations. In his hand, Krishna was clutching butter and rice, which he was tasting, and from his neck swung a garland of forest flowers. The fortunate pilgrim saw the forest of Vrindavan surrounding Krishna, in which cows grazed peacefully and birds called from the branches of the trees. As he gazed upon this vision he could not hold back his tears, which flowed down his cheeks as he shivered in ecstasy. He fainted, and when he came to, he saw Nimai in front of him.

"I have shown you this vision of myself, because for many lifetimes you have been my faithful devotee," said Nimai. "In a previous birth you were a guest of my father, Nanda Maharaj, in Vrindavan. At that time, the same thing happened and I ate your offering. Now I live here in Navadvip. Here I will show everyone my favor by blessing them with love for God. You may stay in

Navadvip and see me regularly, but you must tell no one of what you have seen and heard tonight—this will remain our secret."

The pilgrim suddenly found himself alone again in the room. In silent ecstasy he ate the food blessed by Nimai, and then slept soundly.

Afterward, he became a regular visitor to Nimai's house. He never left Navadvip, and his story remained a secret for many years.

Mischievous Child

When Nimai was old enough to begin school, a ceremony was held to mark his passage into boyhood. The custom was to cut a boy's hair, chant verses from the Vedic hymns, and introduce him to writing the letters of the alphabet.

Jagannath gave his son a slate and a piece of chalk and guided his hand to form the letters of the Bengali alphabet for the first time. As he did so, he pronounced each letter, "ka, kha, ga, gha," and Nimai repeated the sounds after him.

Nimai took delight in making the sounds and learned how to write each letter on his first attempt. Within two or three days he had mastered the whole alphabet. Day and night he would write out the names of God, while chanting them aloud: "Rama, Krishna, Murari, Mukunda." So began Nimai's schooling.

He quickly made friends with his classmates and became their leader. He was a high-spirited child and loved to start logical debates, which he always won. Wherever he was, there was sure to be trouble, and soon he gained a reputation as a naughty boy. Yet, despite his unruly behavior, everybody loved him.

Sometimes, when he could not have what he wanted, Nimai became frustrated. He tried to catch birds, but they always flew away. He longed to reach the moon and stars, demanding, "Give, give!" and cried inconsolably when he could not have them.

At such times, someone would start to chant Krishna's names, and others would follow, dancing and clapping their hands. Then Nimai would suddenly be happy again.

One afternoon after school, Nimai was playing by the Ganges with his friends. The *brahmanas* of Navadvip gathered there every day to chant mantras and perform rituals. Nimai liked to tease them. After they bathed, he threw dust over them, so they would have to wash themselves again in the river, and while they were in the water he splashed them. The more they forbade him, the more he ignored their protests. Finally, they would lose their patience and complain to his father. On one occasion a delegation went to see Jagannath.

"Jagannath Mishra, please do something about Nimai. When we chant mantras to Vishnu, your son interrupts us and claims *he* is Vishnu. He takes our offerings meant for Vishnu, and says, 'Why are you troubled? I am the one you worship.' We try to catch him, but he retreats into the water, where he floats for hours with his friends, splashing us if we come near. You must discipline your child." They spoke angrily, but really they loved Nimai and did not want him to come to any harm.

The village girls were often by the Ganges, and they too were unhappy with Nimai, for he teased them as well. Some of them complained to his mother: "Sachi, your son insults us, splashes us, and steals our clothes while we are bathing. When we make offerings of flowers and fruits, he spoils them, and after we finish bathing and are clean, he throws sand over us. None of us like him. Please stop him or we will report him to our parents." Although they said this, the girls all loved Nimai.

Hearing these complaints, Jagannath set off for the riverside with his stick, determined to deal with his disobedient son.

This made the girls sorry, and they ran ahead to warn Nimai that his father was coming. After making his friends promise to say that they had not seen him at the Ganges that day, Nimai ran off. By the time Jagannath arrived, he was nowhere to be found.

"Nimai didn't come here today," his friends chorused. "He must have gone straight home from school by the other path."

The *brahmanas* were more truthful, but they also spoke up for Nimai.

"We saw him here, but he ran away in fear," they said. "Don't be angry with him, Jagannath—just give him a good talking to. We all love him and think you are truly fortunate to have such a spirited and intelligent son." They embraced Jagannath and calmed him down, so he returned to his house feeling reassured. Just as Jagannath returned, Nimai arrived home, apparently from school, covered in dust, carrying his school books, and with his fingers marked with ink.

"Mother," he cried, "I have been working hard at school all day. Now I need to go to the Ganges to bathe." Jagannath looked at Nimai with surprise.

"What are you up to, Nimai?" his father demanded to know. "You are upsetting everyone at the Ganges."

"Father, they all make up stories about me," complained Nimai. "I haven't even been to the Ganges today." Smiling, and without waiting for an answer, the laughing boy ran off to join his friends by the river, where they gathered around to praise his bold escape. At home, his parents were left bewildered.

"Surely all these people would not lie about Nimai," reasoned Jagannath. "Yet he can't have bathed already—his hair was dry, and dust and ink stains covered his body. Who is this child of ours, who at once enchants and maddens everyone? He must be someone special. Perhaps Krishna himself has been born among us." Thus their hearts filled with love and endless bliss.

Loss of a Brother and a Father

As a young schoolboy, Nimai grew in confidence and authority. He would listen to no one—not his teacher, nor his mother, nor even his father. But one person commanded his respect—his older brother, Vishvarup, to whom Nimai was devoted. Vishvarup possessed a natural authority and, at the same time, a gentle nature that made him loved and respected by all. He was always studying the *Srimad Bhagavatam*, which told the stories of Krishna. Regularly he gave discourse on spiritual topics.

One day, Vishvarup visited Advaita Acharya's house in Navadvip, where the Vaishnavas were gathered to hear about Krishna and chant his names. Despite his youth, Vishvarup was deeply learned and devoted to God. He attracted everyone present with his accounts of Krishna and his explanations of spiritual life. Absorbed in his meditations and enjoying the spiritual company, he forgot to return home for supper. Meanwhile, his mother waited for him.

"Go and fetch your brother," she told Nimai. The young boy ran off to bring his older brother home. Soon, Nimai arrived breathless and excited at Advaita's house.

"Mother wants you to come home and eat," exclaimed Nimai, tugging at his brother's clothes. He did not notice that he had become the center of attention. The Vaishnavas had heard about Nimai, but had not seen him. Now that they saw him they were struck by the child's beauty and spiritual effulgence. They wondered what it was about him that so captivated them. None of them suspected that the reason they were drawn to him might be that he was Krishna, soul of souls, the very one to whom they daily prayed.

On this occasion, Vishvarup obediently accompanied Nimai home, but increasingly he spent time away in the company of devotees. He wanted only to hear about Krishna, and family life held no attraction for him. Even when he was at home, he usually confined himself to the shrine room and was rarely to be seen.

When he was twelve, Vishvarup overheard his parents planning his marriage. This filled him with dismay. He had but one desire—to devote himself to God. Marriage held no attraction for him. He lay awake that night wondering what to do and finally decided to leave home to become a wandering monk. The very next day he left and traveled to South India, where he spent the remainder of his life on perpetual pilgrimage from one holy place to another.

When their eldest son left them, Sachi and Jagannath were distraught. Day and night they wept, and could not be consoled. Nimai, who had been devoted to his older brother, was deeply affected. His hero and inspiration had abandoned him and gone to be a *sannyasi*, a traveling monk, who had renounced all ties with his family. This experience made an indelible impression on his young heart and he resolved that one day he would follow in his brother's footsteps. However, Nimai knew that for now his parents needed him more than ever, and he must take Vishvarup's place at home. Thus, he decided to become serious about his studies and abandoned his mischievous play.

Nimai threw himself into his schoolwork and scriptural studies. So sharp was his intellect that upon once hearing a verse from any text he would know it by heart. His knowledge rapidly increased until no one could defeat him in debate.

"Jagannath Mishra, you are a lucky man to have such a gifted son," people would tell his father. But now a new fear took root in Jagannath's heart: suppose Nimai learned all the scriptures, as Vishvarup had, would he not reach the same conclusion that family life was a distraction, and leave home to follow his brother's example? As a result, to everyone's dismay, Jagannath forbade his son to study.

"Without being educated, how will our boy earn a living?" protested Sachi. "Who will want their daughter to marry him?"

"Being well educated has not earned me a decent living," said Jagannath. "Krishna will look after Nimai as he looks after us all."

Nimai obeyed his father. But without his studies, he was bored and unhappy. He returned to his mischievous ways, teasing the girls, fighting the boys, and playing pranks on the grownups. Soon everyone was begging Jagannath to let his son study again.

"You are lucky to have a son who wants to study," they said, "You should be encouraging him, not holding him back."

Jagannath relented and accepted their advice. A ceremony was held in which Jagannath offered Nimai the sacred thread—a symbol of second birth as a *brahmana* who studies spiritual knowledge—and enrolled him as a student under the learned teacher Gangadas Pandit. Nimai was happy again, and became inseparable from his books. He promised his father that he need not worry; he would not leave home. He would be a dutiful son and look after his parents.

One day, Nimai had a dream. His brother Vishvarup took him by the hand and led him away, telling him to become a *sannyasi*, just as Vishvarup had done. In his dream, Nimai protested, "Our parents are helpless without me. I must stay and serve them." So Vishvarup sent him back home with messages of love for their mother. When he awoke, Nimai told her of his dream.

Jagannath also had a dream. He saw his beloved Nimai grown into an adult, with shaven head, dressed as a *sannyasi*. Surrounding him were thousands of followers whom he led in singing the names of Krishna, while passing through many towns and villages. Jagannath's heart overflowed with happiness to see his son so loved and inspired, but at the same time he was anxious—he did not want to lose his second son to a life of renunciation. When he awoke he prayed fervently to Lord Krishna.

"We are your servants, Lord, and whatever we have is yours. But please protect our son, and do not take him from us."

Shortly thereafter, the saintly Jagannath Mishra, in whose home Krishna secretly played as a child, was taken from this world. His community gathered on the bank of the Ganges to cremate his body. As they watched his ashes merge with the river, Nimai and Sachi wept bitter tears.

In the coming years, Nimai never left his mother's side, and she watched over him constantly. She gazed at her son's moonlike face and forgot her grief. To her, Nimai was everything.

Restless Spirit

Nimai became Sachi's entire world. As he matured, he became a devoted son and dedicated student, and because he exhibited such goodness, she gave him everything he asked for. His father had been there to guide and instruct Nimai, and his elder brother had always been his inspiration and confidential friend. Now they were both gone. Nimai missed their reassuring presence, and there were times when frustrations overcame him when his mother simply could not pacify him.

It was Nimai's custom each day to take a garland of flowers to offer Mother Ganges before bathing in her sacred waters. One day, as usual, he asked Sachi for the garland.

"Just wait and I will bring it to you," she replied.

But when he heard her say "just wait," he lost his patience. The sorrow and frustration stored in his heart since the death of his father burst forth, and he was overcome by sudden rage. He ran inside the house in a reckless mood and began to pull things off shelves. Clay pots stood in a row, holding Ganges water, milk, oil, ghee, salt, and spices. He smashed them all. When he ran out of containers to break, he ripped open sacks of rice, flour, and grains, and scattered their contents on the floor. He tore apart clothes until every garment was in tatters. Still his anger was not quenched, so he turned upon the house itself. Wielding a heavy stick, he beat the fragile mud and bamboo structure and tore at its thatched roof.

With the house reduced to ruins and all within destroyed, he threw himself upon the bare earth and began rolling and beating the ground, crying hot tears of rage. His terrified mother, at a safe distance, could only watch him writhe in the dirt, until at last, his anger spent, exhausted and soaked in tears, he fell asleep stretched out upon the earth. Timidly, Sachi stepped forward, and while he slept she massaged his body, gently wiping away his tears and cleansing the dust from his skin. Then at last she brought the garland and laid it beside him.

After some time Nimai opened his eyes and saw the garland. He smiled at Sachi. A terrible storm had passed and the sun had returned. He picked himself up, took the garland, and without a word walked to the Ganges. While he was gone Sachi cleared a space, and with some ingredients borrowed from her neighbors cooked their lunch. Nimai returned and ate in silence. Without a word he gathered together his books and left for school, where he spent the remainder of the day with his class friends as if nothing had happened.

At the end of the day, Nimai came home and called out to his mother.

"Mother dear, take these and restore everything." He pressed into her hands two gold coins. "Krishna provides all our needs," he said. "We will never want for anything." Without further explanation, he went to bed.

Sachi could not understand why her son had behaved as he did, nor where he had acquired the gold. Whatever he did, she accepted, as Mother Earth tolerates her children. Cautiously, she took the coins and showed them to her friends. Receiving their assurances that she should use the gold to restore their house, she replaced everything as it had been before.

·······

AT SCHOOL NIMAI SURPASSED EVERYONE in his studies of Sanskrit grammar and logic. Although he was the youngest of Gangadas's students, he was soon able to defeat in argument even the senior pupil, Murari Gupta. Navadvip teemed with students of the various academies. When each day ended, they congregated by the Ganges and played games, splashing and fighting in the water, challenging each other in verbal contests, always vying to see who was the strongest and cleverest.

Nimai knew no fear. Without hesitation he would go up to a group of older boys and challenge them.

"Why are you so arrogant and always picking fights?" they demanded to know. "Do you think you are better than us?"

"Ask me any question and see," laughed Nimai. They would try to get the better of him, but none of them could. First, he would perfectly explain some particular point in a way they couldn't refute; then he would take the opposite position and disprove his own argument. By doing this he overcame them all, even his elders. Yet none of them minded being beaten by him. Instead they embraced him and made him their leader.

Nimai was an unusually beautiful youth with black curly hair and deep smiling eyes. He had stature and presence and walked with power and grace. When he passed by, everyone was attracted to him, and wherever he went, he was surrounded by friends and admirers. He never spoke of Krishna. Who would understand? The people were preoccupied with materialism and were not ready to hear about such things.

Only the Vaishnavas who met at Advaita's house followed the spiritual path and were devoted to Krishna. But they felt outnumbered and misunderstood. People mocked them for their constant singing of Krishna's names, and thought them to be sentimental fools. One day, Advaita spoke words of encouragement to his friends.

"Do not despair, Krishna will help us. I feel in my heart that he is with us." In response, the Vaishnavas continued to trust in Krishna's protection and to sing his names, "Hari! Hari!"

Nimai happened to be nearby with his friends. He heard them calling the name of Hari and came running to Advaita's house.

"Why have you come, my child?" asked the adults.

"Why did you call me?" responded Nimai.

They didn't understand that he had come in answer to hearing them sing his name, and he ran off to play again with his friends.

The Bank of the Ganges

At the age of sixteen, Nimai was head of his household. He cared for his mother and worked hard at his studies so that he could soon begin teaching to support the home. Custom required a young man in his position to have a wife. Wishing to fulfill the duties expected of him, despite his youth, Nimai began to think of marriage.

One day on the way home from school, he met Lakshmidevi, daughter of a local *brahmana*. They were each following the path along the bank of the Ganges when they came face to face.

This was not their first encounter. When he was younger, Nimai delighted in teasing the girls by the river. Sometimes they collected flowers and fruits to offer to the goddess Durga, praying for her help in finding future husbands. Nimai used to disrupt their worship. He would take their offerings for himself, and playfully give them his blessings.

"If you worship me, I promise you will find handsome and intelligent husbands, and each of you will be blessed with seven sons and prosperous homes." The girls liked what he said, but pretending to be angry they ran away.

"If you don't worship me," he would call after them, "you will end up marrying old men and having to live with many co-wives." Hearing this, the girls were afraid, so they ran back to receive Nimai's blessings. Among these girls was one whom Nimai liked. She only came once to pray for a husband, and although they were both still young children, a bond formed between them on that day.

"Worship me, and I promise I will fulfill all your desires," Nimai had told her, and she had devotedly given him all her offerings intended for Durga. That girl was Lakshmidevi.

Now they met again, on the path by the Ganges, not far from where they had first found each other. They smiled in recognition. Love awakened, and in their hearts they accepted one another as partners.[8]

Among the *brahmana* community of Navadvip was a matchmaker named Vanamali. He always had his ear to the ground and knew who was ready to be married. His heart told him to speak with Sachi about her son.

"I know of a suitable match for Nimai," he confided. "Her name is Lakshmidevi, daughter of Vallabha Acharya. Why don't you get them married?"

Sachi was hesitant. Although she knew her son must now become a grownup householder, she didn't want to lose her little Nimai. So, after listening to Vanamali, she sent him away without an answer. Nimai, however, heard that the matchmaker had visited and was pleased. He spoke to his mother, encouraging her to call Vanamali again. Once Sachi knew Nimai's mind, her hesitation was gone. She told Vanamali to go ahead with the arrangement without delay. In time-honored fashion, the matchmaker called on Lakshmidevi's father and greeted him with respect.

"The son of the noble Jagannath Mishra is a gifted and saintly young man. He would be an excellent husband for your daughter. What do you say?"

Vallabha was overjoyed at this suggestion, but one thing troubled him.

"I am embarrassed that I can't afford a dowry. All I can afford are fruits and flowers. Please ask Sachi if this is acceptable."

Sachi did not care about Vallabha's modest circumstances. She was only concerned that he was a good man, and happy that his daughter would marry her son. So the marriage was agreed upon, and an auspicious date was set according to astrological calculations.

On the eve of this momentous day, they held a ceremony at Nimai's house, with the bride's father present. They chanted prayers and offered a garland to the groom, while musicians and dancers entertained their guests.

Early the next morning, while last-minute preparations were under way, the whole neighborhood gathered to celebrate the marriage of their much-loved Nimai. As the auspicious hour of sunset approached, Nimai, dressed in new cloth and decorated with a fresh garland, accompanied his mother to Vallabha Acharya's house. Vallabha received his son-in-law with respect, offered him a seat, and then presented Lakshmidevi to him. While everyone chanted the names of Krishna, the bride walked around her husband seven times and prayed to Vishnu for his future health and happiness. Then they held hands and were venerated by the whole assembly, according to Bengali custom. Joy was felt by all in attendance.

That night, the couple stayed at the bride's house, attended by her girlfriends, and the next day Nimai brought his wife home, where further festivities were held. The couple possessed such an aura of beauty and grace that people thought they were witnessing Vishnu and his eternal consort, the goddess Lakshmi herself.

Master of Navadvip

The newly married couple settled into Sachi's home and all looked after each other. Nimai's home life took on a gentler mood with Lakshmidevi at his side. For Sachi, life was transformed. Nimai's young wife seemed to bestow light and comfort on all who associated with her. Sometimes Sachi fancied she saw a glowing flame next to her son, but upon looking again she realized it was Lakshmidevi. Similarly, she often smelled the aroma of fresh lotus flowers pervading the house. After a while, she concluded that this girl must be the Goddess of Fortune, come to live with her and her son, and that this was why they no longer experienced poverty.

Nimai regularly withdrew in silence to the shrine room, and when he did Sachi imagined that she heard celestial flute music from inside the room. She also saw supernatural light spilling from his doorway to fill the house. Sometimes, she heard heavenly singing and the tinkling ankle bells of unseen dancers, or she glimpsed luminous figures entering her home to pay homage. At these times, she shivered and her eyes glistened with tears.

In scholarship Nimai surpassed all others. He had long overtaken his fellow older pupils, and even his teachers could not better his knowledge of Sanskrit grammar. One day a well-to-do citizen of Navadvip, Mukunda-Sanjaya, invited Nimai to teach his son. Others became Nimai's students as well. Murari Gupta had been a school friend of Nimai's. The two of them had often debated points of grammar, and although Murari was older and more educated, Nimai always won the argument. Now Murari was a doctor and he wanted to learn Sanskrit. He approached Nimai.

"Please let me be your student," he submitted, and Nimai happily agreed.

Soon other students asked if they too could join Nimai's classes. One of them was Mukunda, another former school friend. He was a gentle soul who loved to sing at the Vaishnava gatherings at Advaita's house. When he sang to Krishna, the devotees' hearts melted and they would openly cry. Besides being Krishna's devotee, Mukunda was an accomplished scholar who was proud of his learning. If Nimai encountered Mukunda on the street, he would challenge him on some point of philosophy, and as usual Nimai would win. Each time this occurred, Mukunda tried to refute Nimai's arguments, but never with any success. Eventually he reached the point that if he saw Nimai approaching, he would run in the opposite direction.

One day, Nimai cornered Mukunda and took him by the hand. "Why do you avoid me?" he asked. "Is it because I don't talk about Krishna?" Saying this, Nimai turned to his friends, and as the students gathered around him he promised, "The time will soon come when I will speak of nothing but Krishna." It was on that day that Mukunda became his student.

Another of Nimai's companions who enrolled as his student was Gadadhar. The two of them became fast friends and remained close for the rest of their lives.

Seeing all these students joining Nimai, the wealthy Mukunda-Sanjaya offered him the spacious veranda in front of his house as a place where he could teach. Thus, Nimai began his teaching career, and his fame spread as Nimai Pandit, the best Sanskrit teacher in Navadvip.

Between classes, Nimai walked around the town with his students, always with a book in his hand. If he met any teachers, he challenged them to a debate. He excelled in all departments of knowledge—grammar, logic, rhetoric, and philosophy—and was quick to prove his mastery.

Although Nimai's behavior might have seemed arrogant, he had a way of gaining his opponent's love and respect. This had a strange effect on scholars. They feared his sharp wit and cutting tongue, but they couldn't help being attracted to him. Consequently, although one by one he defeated them all, he made no enemies in Navadvip.

At the end of each day, Nimai went to the water's edge, where he sat on the bathing *ghats*, illuminated by the setting sun and surrounded by students and admirers. All who looked at him wondered at his beauty and learning, while those who were Vaishnavas secretly prayed for him to become a full-fledged devotee of Krishna.

One of Nimai's friends was a poor banana seller named Kolavecha Shridhar. It was Nimai's habit to tease shopkeepers to see how much he could talk them into giving him. He would go from one stallholder to another in the marketplace, and invariably walk away with gifts. Frequently, he visited Shridhar's banana stall on the edge of the marketplace. Shridhar was a poor man whose main activity was prayer. He owned a small banana plantation and made a meager living selling his produce, patiently accepting whatever little he earned as the blessings of God. Nimai, smartly dressed in silk robes and ornaments, used to joke with Shridhar about his worn clothing and ramshackle house. He always made a point of begging bananas from him, even though he knew Shridhar couldn't afford to give anything away. Shridhar was glad to feed Nimai, and gave his goods to him with genuine love. The two of them, although so different, became close friends.

·······

ONE DAY, NIMAI PANDIT ASKED an astrologer to give him a reading.

"I have heard that you know everything," said Nimai. "Tell me who I was in my previous birth."

The astrologer meditated and saw a vision of Vishnu, the soul of the universe. It seemed to him that the one standing before him was that same divine person. At first he was speechless. Nimai waited to hear his conclusion.

"By my calculations, in your previous birth you were the shelter of the universe," he finally said, "and you are still that same person."

When Nimai heard this he smiled.

"You are mistaken. I know that in my last birth I was a cowherd boy, and because I looked after cows I have now been rewarded with birth as a *brahmana*."

"Whatever you are, I offer you my respects," was all the astrologer could reply.

Youthful Success

Early each morning Nimai Pandit met his class in the courtyard in front of Mukunda-Sanjaya's house. Lessons lasted until noon when they all swam in the Ganges. Nimai then went home to worship Vishnu and have lunch followed by a short nap. In the afternoon, books in hand, he strolled around the town, where he would stop and chat with friends, laughing and joking as admirers gathered around him.

Eventually he made his way to the bathing *ghats*, where he again met his students. Sitting in their midst, like the moon surrounded by stars, he lectured, first proving a point, then disproving it, then proving it again. No other *pandit* could match him. People watched and listened in awe.

"Is this a demigod come to live among us?" they asked. "Or is he an incarnation of Vishnu? We have heard that one day a *brahmana* will become King of Bengal. Perhaps this is he, for he has all the signs of a king."

The scene was just like the ancient stories of Krishna, who sat by the river Yamuna among his cowherd boyfriends, all of them laughing and joking, and looking upon Krishna with love. Just as those cowherd boys felt indescribable happiness, so did the students who surrounded Nimai Pandit.

One day, a famous *pandit* arrived in Navadvip. He had the title Digvijaya, which means "champion." His intellect and learning was such that he believed himself invincible in argument. Wherever he traveled he challenged local scholars to debate, and in the process won considerable wealth. Digvijaya Pandit paraded into town with a procession of attendants on horses and elephants.

The *pandit* issued a challenge: the scholars of Navadvip should either put forward someone capable of competing with him in debate, or give him a certificate stating that he had defeated them all. When Nimai Pandit heard this news from his students, he smiled to himself and began to think how to defeat this overly proud man; but he wanted to do it without causing him public humiliation.

"The man's reputation should not be destroyed, only his pride," Nimai confided to Gadadhar. "I will try to meet him privately."

That evening, as Nimai taught by the Ganges under a full moon, Digvijaya Pandit approached. He had heard of Nimai Pandit and was curious to meet him. Hearing Nimai speak so eloquently, he realized he was in the presence of a rare genius, and sat down quietly at a distance. Nimai saw him and paused. He greeted him respectfully, then invited the champion scholar to entertain them all with some verses in praise of the Ganges. The *pandit* accepted the invitation to show off his skills. He possessed a special gift: he could spontaneously compose perfect Sanskrit poetry. Without hesitation he stood up, and for three hours glorified the Ganges, chanting Sanskrit verses with ease. His audience was held spellbound. At last he ended, and Nimai thanked him.

"Your verses are wonderful," Nimai said graciously. Then he added with a smile, "But they are difficult for us to understand. Please explain their meaning."

As soon as the learned man began his response, Nimai interrupted.

"One of your verses, however, contained five faults." He quoted the precise verse and explained the errors. He then asked the *pandit* to elucidate.

Digvijaya Pandit was taken aback. How could Nimai select and remember a single verse from a three-hour discourse? He tried to explain the verse in question, but found himself lost for words—Nimai had correctly pointed out clear mistakes in both grammar and logic. Embarrassed by this uncharacteristic carelessness, the great Digvijaya lapsed into an awkward silence.

Some of Nimai's students began to murmur, but he quickly silenced them. He had defeated the *pandit*, but had no wish to make a spectacle of him: for such a proud man, public humiliation would be unbearable.

"You must be tired after your journey. Why don't you rest for the night and tomorrow we can meet and discuss everything."

Digvijaya gladly left and retreated to his lodgings in a thoughtful mood. He was a devoted worshiper of Sarasvati, the Goddess of Learning, and regarded her as the source of his strength. He thought he must have displeased her, and that was why she had allowed his defeat by a mere boy. That night, when he prayed to Sarasvati, she appeared to him in a dream.

"The boy who defeated you is Vishnu, master of countless universes. Before him I am powerless," spoke the merciful goddess. "I am revealing to you this secret because of your sincere devotion to me. Now go quickly and surrender to him."

In the morning, Digvijaya hurried back to Nimai. "I did not recognize you," he said, humbled now, and bowing at Nimai's feet. "I beg your mercy."

"Do not talk like this," protested Nimai. "You are a great *brahmana* and have no need to bow before me."

"The Goddess came to me last night and told me you are Vishnu himself. I only wish that you teach me how to be free from material attachments."

"The only knowledge truly worth possessing is to know that Krishna is the source of all happiness, and to know how to serve him. Abandon your wealth and pride, and surrender to him," replied Nimai. Then he made Digvijaya promise not to reveal to anyone what he had learned about Nimai's true identity.

Digvijaya, like others overcome by Nimai in debate, did not grudge his defeat. His heart had been won over and his life transformed. He gave away his elephants and let his servants go, wanting to travel as a lone mendicant devoted to Krishna. Following this incident Nimai Pandit's fame spread far and wide, and he was proclaimed a lion among debaters. But no one knew who he really was.

········

AROUND THIS TIME, A VAISHNAVA MONK NAMED ISHVARA PURI visited Navadvip. While there, he stayed with Vaishnava families and encouraged them in their devotion. Several times Nimai invited Ishvara to eat at his house, and they spent long hours talking about Krishna. Ishvara was an ecstatic devotee, and whenever he spoke of Krishna his eyes filled with tears. Thus, Nimai became attached to Ishvara. Once, when they were in discussion, Ishvara corrected Nimai on a point of grammar, and Nimai happily accepted the correction. No one else had ever successfully corrected him like this. From that day onward, Nimai began to look upon Ishvara Puri as his teacher, and both he and Gadadhar shared a love for him.

Another devotee who began to influence Nimai was Shrivas, one of the leading Vaishnavas of Navadvip. He was a friend of Advaita Acharya, and he held regular prayer meetings in his house, to which Advaita sometimes came. With interest and concern, Shrivas watched Nimai's growing success.

"Why spend all your time lecturing and studying books," chided Shrivas. "You know these things are vanity. If you are truly learned, you will worship Krishna and teach others to do the same."

"For a little while longer I must carry on my studies," replied Nimai. "Then by your mercy I will become a devotee of Krishna."

Travels

Frequent visitors to Navadvip spread Nimai's reputation as a teacher to neighboring villages. Students came from East Bengal to study under him, and some, after learning his commentaries, shared them with others. Appreciating this, Nimai decided to embark on a teaching tour of East Bengal. Leaving his mother in the care of Lakshmidevi, he set off with a group of friends and students.

As he traveled from village to village, people gathered to see him, and his fame grew. Attracted by his knowledge and commanding personality, many became his students. During this tour he started teaching people to chant the names of Krishna, as he had first done in his childhood. The impression he created on those who met him left a lasting attachment in their hearts, and many became devoted Vaishnavas.

Among these was a young *brahmana* named Tapan Mishra, who was searching for the truth. Although he had studied many books, his heart was not satisfied. He was told in a dream that Nimai Pandit was the person who would enlighten him, and so he set out to find him. One day, while Nimai was teaching Sanskrit in the shadow of a banyan tree, Tapan Mishra came before him and prostrated himself on the ground, begging Nimai to become his spiritual teacher. Nimai's other students were mainly interested in acquiring a material education, but in Mishra, Nimai recognized a sincere seeker of truth.

"In this confused age the best spiritual practice is to chant the holy names of Krishna," said Nimai. "Seek the company of devotees, and chant Krishna's names together. Your love for God will grow and you will find lasting happiness."

Hearing these words, Tapan Mishra became the first to receive Nimai's spiritual teachings. He wanted to join Nimai immediately and return with him to Navadvip. But Nimai had a different idea. Soon he would start his spiritual mission, and this young *brahmana* could help him prepare for the future.

"I want you to go to the holy city of Varanasi," he told Tapan Mishra. "Settle there with your family and wait for me. I promise I will come there and teach you the goal of life."

Varanasi, on the banks of the Ganges about five hundred miles upriver to the west, was North India's greatest center of spiritual learning. It was Nimai's plan to one day visit that city and instruct its spiritual leaders. Tapan would go ahead to prepare the way. Nimai gave his young disciple a warm embrace and the two parted.

········

At home in Navadvip, Lakshmidevi missed her husband greatly. Each night she lay awake, her eyes filled with tears, thinking of her beloved. Two months passed without news of his return. Weakened by loss of appetite, she could bear their separation no longer and lost the will to live without him. She sat beside the Ganges, meditating on Nimai's feet with determination, and left this world behind.[9]

Lakshmidevi's death was a deep shock to everyone, especially Sachi, who was left all alone. Her tears flowed day and night and were pitiful for her friends to behold.

Unaware of these events, Nimai brought his travels to an end and turned homeward. When his newly acquired students heard he was leaving, many of them decided to go with him to continue their studies. So it was that, after two months of traveling and teaching, Nimai returned to Navadvip with a large retinue, bearing valuable gifts he had received from the people of East Bengal.

Late one afternoon, Nimai and his party arrived in Navadvip. His friends greeted him with celebration and joy, not knowing how to tell him the sad news. According to tradition, they took him to the Ganges for his customary bath after a long journey. He assumed that his mother and wife were home cooking a feast for him, as they had often done before. His friends dreaded having to tell him of Lakshmidevi's death. When all the festivities were over and the others were taking their leave, Nimai was finally able to go inside his house to greet the two women he had missed so much. He found only Sachi, weeping.

"Mother, what is the matter—are you not pleased to see me?"

Sachi could not answer.

"Where is Lakshmidevi?" he cried, and at last a friend uttered the unspeakable. "O Nimai, your dear wife went to the Ganges and has not returned."

Hearing these words, Nimai remained motionless. For a while, soft tears glided down his golden cheeks. Then, recollecting himself and the wisdom of the *Vedas*, he embraced his sorrowing mother and consoled her with comforting words.

"By the will of Vishnu we are brought together and imagine ourselves related as sons and mothers, or husbands and wives, and by his will we are again parted. Since it is his wish for the fortunate Lakshmidevi to reach the Ganges before her husband, we need not be sad."

Her son's calm words helped Sachi regain her composure. She still had him, and that was what mattered most. As long as Nimai was with her she could weather any storm. With his support, she called their friends and relatives, and together they performed the rituals for Lakshmidevi's departed soul. In due course, as the sun returns north from its southward journey, happiness returned to their hearts.

Remarriage

Bereft of the companionship of his young wife, Nimai threw himself with renewed energy into his teaching. His inclination toward spiritual life and plans for teaching it were a secret confided only to a few trusted friends. Externally he maintained his outgoing, sociable nature, but privately he began to change.

He became strict in his religious observance—in his daily meditation and worship at home—and he expected his students to be strict in their meditations as well. He insisted that they wear the sign of Vishnu on their foreheads and give proper attention to their own daily observances. He also no longer joked with the girls of Navadvip. As a boy he loved to tease them by the Ganges, but from now on he preserved a respectful distance. This reserve toward women remained a feature of his life forever after.

His new seriousness was in marked contrast with his former high spirits and playful ways. The people of Navadvip noticed these changes and wondered where they would lead.

········

SACHI SAW HER SON'S ABSORPTION IN HIS WORK and understood that, at least in part, it was because he missed his wife. She wanted to resolve this problem and see him settled in household life. Accordingly, after some time, she asked him to consider a new bride. To please his mother, he agreed. Sachi had noticed a *brahmana* girl named Vishnupriya who was devoted to the Ganges and respectful to her superiors. She seemed an ideal match for her son. Sachi sent a message to the girl's father, the wealthy *brahmana* Sanatan Mishra, requesting his daughter's hand for Nimai. After discussing the idea with his family, the *brahmana* gladly accepted the proposal.

A rich man of Navadvip named Buddhimanta Khan, who was an admirer of Nimai and knew that his family did not have much money, offered to sponsor a wedding festival of royal proportions.

On the eve of the wedding day, two celebrations were held, one for Nimai at his home, and one for Vishnupriya at her home. The men and women of the town offered the betrothed their blessings. According to local custom, the many *brahmanas* of Navadvip were invited and showered with gifts and sumptuously fed.

As the wedding day dawned, Nimai went to the Ganges to bathe. During the morning, Sachi visited her relatives to offer them gifts of fruit, ghee, and grains. All over town houses were decorated with waterpots, flags, and mango leaves. In the afternoon, Nimai dressed in a new yellow *dhoti*, put on gold earrings, a jeweled necklace, and a crown, and decorated his face with sandalwood paste, black eye ointment, and the sign of Vishnu on his forehead.

A grand procession set off through the town that afternoon toward the bride's house. Nimai was carried by his friends in a palanquin, surrounded by women singing auspicious mantras. Lamp carriers walked ahead and on either side, followed by dancers, musicians, and flag bearers. Children ran alongside, and everyone danced, even the elders of the town. The procession passed along the bank of the Ganges, then through the center of Navadvip until, just as the sun was setting, it reached Sanatan Mishra's palatial house. He greeted Nimai and took him inside, where the women of the family offered him gifts and worshipped him with lamps.

When all the guests were seated, with Nimai in the center, Vishnupriya appeared. She walked around her husband seven times to honor him, then offered a garland at his feet, which he in turn placed around her neck. They sat side by side while their guests showered them with flowers. Priests chanted mantras and lit a sacred fire, and everyone enjoyed a wedding feast. After the festivities, the bride and groom retired to spend their first night together as guests in her father's house.

The following day, a procession led the couple back through the streets to Nimai's house, with more chanting, music, and celebrations. There, Nimai distributed gifts to the poor, and to all who had helped.

Nimai's first wedding to Lakshmidevi had been a small family affair. Now, two years later, the whole town joined him to celebrate his wedding to Vishnupriya. He turned to Buddhimanta Khan, whose generosity had paid for the festival, and embraced him with warmth and gratitude. Although he was not yet eighteen years old, Nimai Pandit had established himself as the leading scholar of Navadvip and had achieved earthly success and fame. However, his destiny lay elsewhere.

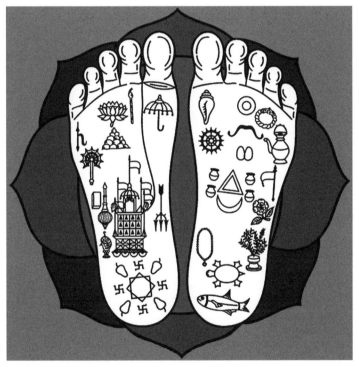

The lotus feet of Sri Chaitanya.

BOOK TWO

The Mission Begins

Spiritual Awakening

Nimai wanted to make the pilgrimage to Gaya in memory of his father. Tradition required a son to make offerings for the soul of his departed father and his ancestors at the great Vishnu temple in Gaya. With this intention, Nimai made preparations and set off, taking some of his students for company. They traveled on foot, following the course of the Ganges upstream from Navadvip.

After several weeks, walking from village to village, they reached the temple in Gaya. Inside the great temple was the "footprint" of Vishnu. The ancient footprint was said to have been made by Vishnu to record his promise that he would honor any offering made to him there on behalf of a deceased soul. To see this footprint was the final object of a pilgrimage to Gaya. Pilgrims entered the Vishnu temple, and after passing through its outer precincts, attended by many priests, they mounted steps to reach the inner shrine room. There, clothed in shadows and illuminated by burning oil lamps, amid much chanting and offering of garlands and incense, was the sacred footprint embedded in a large black stone.

When Nimai gazed at Vishnu's footprint, he was overcome by a flood of emotion. His eyes filled with tears, his body shivered, and he almost fell to the ground in a state of ecstasy. His companions had no idea what to do. This was the first time they had witnessed these manifestations of Nimai's deep love for Krishna. They were unaware that from this time on such signs would become an ever-present part of his life.

Helped by his friends, Nimai recovered his composure and together they left the temple. As they emerged, Nimai recognized a familiar face. It was

Ishvara Puri, the teacher who had stayed in Navadvip and given instruction to Nimai and Gadadhar. He too was visiting Gaya. Without hesitation, Nimai prostrated himself before the devout *brahmana* and rose to embrace him with affection.

"I came here to pray for the deliverance of my ancestors," said Nimai. "Now I have found you, who have the power to deliver us all from birth and death. Please grant me the gift of Krishna's lotus feet."

"Dear Nimai, you yourself must be Krishna," replied Ishvara Puri. "For since I first saw you I can think only of Him."

Nimai smiled, saying, "I am fortunate to find you, my dear friend."

The two parted for the rest of that day. Nimai, with his companions, visited the sacred sites of Gaya where he made offerings for his ancestors, then returned a second time to worship Vishnu's footprint. At the end of the day, they came back to their guest house and Nimai cooked everyone a meal. As he was about to sit down and eat, Ishvara Puri arrived to see him. Nimai insisted on giving him the meal he had kept for himself; then he cooked again. When they had both finished eating, Nimai made sure Ishvara Puri was comfortable. Wishing to honor him as his teacher, Nimai served him by massaging his feet with fragrant oil.

"Now that I have met you and served your feet, my visit to Gaya is successful," he said.

For some days Nimai stayed on in Gaya in the company of Ishvara Puri and considered what to do. When Nimai had seen Vishnu's footprint, his spiritual feelings had awakened in the most unexpected way, and now he could think of nothing but Krishna's lotus feet. He felt it was time for him to take an important step. And providence had sent at this precise moment the perfect person to help him. Humbly, he approached Ishvara Puri and asked for mantra initiation.

"I give my body in your service. Please bless me with love for Krishna," prayed Nimai. Ishvara Puri accepted Nimai as his disciple and gave him the ten-syllable mantra made up of names of Krishna. Again the two embraced, crying tears of love. Thus Nimai received initiation. On that day, he accepted Ishvara Puri as his spiritual master and forever remained devoted to him. Later in life he always carried with him a small bag of dust taken from Ishvara Puri's birthplace, and told his intimate friends that this dust, and the bond it signified, was what kept him alive.

The next day, Nimai went alone to a quiet place and settled to meditate on the mantra he had been given. As soon as he chanted Krishna's names, he entered a deep trance and saw Krishna. When he emerged from his meditation, the vision of Krishna vanished and Nimai cried aloud.

"O Krishna, my dear father. O my life, Lord Hari. Where have you gone?" Falling to the ground in distress, he called again and again for Krishna. His students came in search of him and found him crying and rolling in the dust. They were alarmed, and did their best to calm him, but he wanted them to leave him.

"Go home," he said. "I can no longer teach you. I must depart immediately for Vrindavan to find Krishna. He is the master of my life."

That very night, when they were all asleep, Nimai started out for Vrindavan, Krishna's childhood home, a month's journey westward. In a state of trance he walked into the night, calling upon Krishna as he went. After some time, he heard a voice from the darkness. "Now is not the time for you to go to Vrindavan. First, you must fulfill your destiny, which is to spread the chanting of Krishna's names everywhere and to teach all souls to love God. Return home and begin your mission. Later you will be able to visit Vrindavan."

Hearing this divine voice, Nimai was consoled. He halted and returned to Gaya. There he found his companions, and together they journeyed back the way they had come. As they traveled, day by day Nimai's feelings intensified and his longing for Krishna grew.

One day, they passed through a village named after Krishna. There Nimai caught sight of a beautiful boy dancing and playing the flute. He was dark-skinned, dressed in a bright yellow *dhoti*, and wearing a necklace of jewels, with a peacock feather decorating his dark, curling hair. The boy ran up to Nimai and embraced him, then darted away. Only Nimai saw this. He was convinced he had seen and touched Krishna. The memory of this vision never left him. Absorbed in this remembrance, always wishing to find Krishna and again feel his embrace, Nimai continued traveling with his friends until they reached Navadvip.

Nimai Pandit's Transformation

Nimai returned a changed person. Gone were his youthful arrogance and playful wit. Instead, his many friends, eager to see him after his absence, found in him an air of introspection and an uncharacteristic modesty. He greeted them quietly as they crowded round to hear his news.

"Let me go inside," he said, excusing himself, and with a few close friends retreated from the crowd.

Once in his room, he told them of the wonders of Gaya, of the great temple and his bliss upon seeing the footprint of Vishnu. But before he could go on to tell them of his fortunate meeting with Ishvara Puri, he started weeping helplessly and calling on Krishna. His friends had not seen him like this before. They felt they were witnessing something important, but none of them knew how to respond. After a while he recovered and asked them to let him rest. Tomorrow at Shuklambar's house, he said, he would speak to them again.

The next morning, Gadadhar and other Vaishnava friends gathered as usual at Shrivas's house. Those who had been with Nimai the night before reported his transformation. When the others heard he was talking constantly of Krishna, they wanted to see him immediately, and quickly made their way to Shuklambar's house to await his arrival.

Nimai entered the room and began talking about Krishna. As he spoke he was once more carried away. He said he had found his Lord in Gaya, but now he had lost him. He was overcome and fell to the ground. The effect on those with him was unexpected; they were moved by his powerful emotions and could not help weeping along with him. After a while Nimai became silent. He sat up and everyone grew still. As he looked around the room, his eyes fell upon a familiar face.

"Gadadhar my friend, you are here. You have always been devoted to Krishna. As for me, I wasted my youth. Now at last I have found the treasure of my life, but because of my sins this treasure has left me." He took Gadadhar's hands in his and appealed, "Can anyone help me find Krishna, and relieve my distress?"

Together they chanted Krishna's name. In turns they cried and laughed, and so passed the whole day.

Word of Nimai's change spread through the small community of Vaishnavas. A wave of hope arose among them. All of Navadvip loved and admired Nimai.

If he joined the Vaishnavas, their fortunes would change; people would take notice and their tradition would be restored. Advaita Acharya, their respected elder, said Nimai's transformation must be the answer to his prayers.

In Nimai's home, however, the mood was different. His mother and wife were alarmed by his sudden change in behavior. Whenever Vishnupriya tried to speak with him, he turned away and called upon Krishna. At night, he kept them awake with his tears, as he cried with spiritual longing for the Lord of his life. Sachi, remembering the loss of her first son, feared Nimai too might leave her to accept a life of renunciation. Understanding her fear, he sat with her and tried to explain. He taught her of the miseries experienced by the soul, trapped in the womb, and how calling upon God gives release from the pains of birth and death.

"Dear mother, this world is full of suffering. The only way to escape the miseries of birth and death is to worship Krishna. Don't you see? I must follow this path with utmost seriousness."

No matter how he tried to encourage her and explain what had happened to him, still she was unhappy at the changes he was going through. She insisted that he return to his teaching work, and sent him to see his old teacher, Gangadas. When he arrived, his teacher was waiting for him.

"You have found great fortune," said Gangadas. "But your students need you. You are their teacher and they depend on you to set a good example. Like everyone in our community, they are devoted to you. Please continue to teach them."

Early the following day, in obedience to his teacher, Nimai went to the Ganges to bathe and wait for his students. They came, books in hand, and begged him to resume teaching. He sat down, with them surrounding him, and began to teach, but he found himself unable to talk of anything other than Krishna. He taught them how all scriptures pointed to Krishna; how Krishna's name was found in every word; how devotion to Krishna was life's greatest treasure and how all else was a distraction. They were enthralled by his words, yet bewildered. He broke off, laughing.

"Forget your studies. Today we will bathe in the Ganges." And there in the waters, glowing with a new beauty they were astonished to see, he played with them as he had always done.

In the days that followed, Nimai regularly met his students and taught them, speaking only of Krishna. They questioned him closely, trying to make him return to his old style of teaching. Yet whatever they asked, he found a way to answer by talking about Krishna. Sometimes he would call out Krishna's name and shiver with ecstasy. Some of them openly said he was crazy; others thought he might be ill. Looking for help, his students turned to Gangadas.

"Nimai Pandit no longer teaches us properly. How will we learn? Please speak to him and find out what's wrong." Hearing this plea, Gangadas called for Nimai.

"I am glad you are now a Vaishnava, Nimai, but please don't stop your teaching. You can be a devotee of Krishna and still carry on your work. It is your duty to help these students complete their studies."

Nimai was respectful to his teacher, so he took these words seriously. Saying he would tell the whole town the true meaning of scripture in such a way that no one could find fault with his teaching, he sat down in the main square and gathered his students round him, like stars surrounding the full moon. There he began to lecture. As he spoke, he proved conclusively, point by point, that Krishna is the essence of everything.

"Krishna's power lives in all bodies as the breath of life," he said. "It is this that we love. When the body dies and Krishna leaves, even if it is the body of my father or mother, I love it no more and burn it to ashes. Therefore, truly it is Krishna whom we all love, all of the time."

He taught in a way they had never heard before, patiently convincing them of Krishna consciousness, putting forward sound and indisputable arguments for every point of philosophy, always reaching the conclusion that they devote themselves to Krishna, who was found in all of life and in every word of scripture.

Many townsfolk came to hear him and listened with rapt attention. Some tried to argue with him, but none could contradict anything he said. As the day passed, he talked on in deep ecstasy. The sun sank beneath the horizon and still his audience listened spellbound.

Late in the evening, a *brahmana* happened by, chanting Sanskrit poetry that described the beauty of Krishna, who wears a garland of forest flowers and has a peacock feather in his hair. Nimai overheard this and lapsed into a trance. As all looked on in wondering silence, he trembled like a leaf and tears poured from his eyes. Gadadhar, who was close beside him, took Nimai in his arms and gently brought him to his senses.

"What happened?" asked Nimai. His shocked students assured him all was well and led him to the Ganges to bathe.

········

EARLY THE NEXT MORNING NIMAI WAS SURPRISED to find his students assembled at his house, carrying their books and patiently waiting for him to teach them. He bathed and dressed, and was soon sitting in their midst. They listened, full of concentration, as he taught them all through the day, explaining how life depends upon Krishna and how Krishna is in everything.

Six hours passed, and not a murmur came from any student. At last he concluded, "As long as you have life in your body, serve Krishna's lotus feet."

He paused and looked closely at each of them.

"What have I been saying these last few days? I cannot remember."

They told him all that had occurred over the last ten days; how he had fallen repeatedly into trance; how he had bewildered them with his explanations; how he had convinced the whole town with his philosophy of Krishna consciousness.

"Why didn't you stop me?" appealed Nimai. "You should have restrained me."

"We were afraid to challenge you," they answered. "You spoke absolute truth which none could contradict."

At last there seemed to be no more to say.

"I must leave you," announced Nimai. "You are free to go to whomever you like. I bless you all to be fearless, to go where your hearts lead you. From now on I can speak only of Krishna." With this, he tied up his bundle of books.

"Now that we have heard you, how can we learn from anyone else?" His students wept. "We will carry your words in our hearts." Then they too tied up their books, as he tearfully embraced them, one by one.

"All of you, take shelter of Krishna and always chant his name."

"But how shall we chant?" they wanted to know.

He taught them a prayer composed of Krishna's names:

hare haraye namah krishna yadavaya namah
gopala govinda rama sri madhusudana

"I offer my respects to Hari, to Krishna, the descendant of King Yadu. O Gopala, Govinda, Rama, O Madhusudana!"

Clapping his hands he started the chant, and they joined in. As the chant grew louder, he became more absorbed, and the singing grew more intense, bringing other people out to see what was happening. From all over Navadvip they flocked to see this wonder. Nimai had become an ecstatic and merciful devotee of Krishna, who would bring hope to the people and lead them in the glorious chanting of Krishna's names. The once proud young *pandit* was transformed into Vishvambhar, "the shelter of all."

From now on, Navadvip would also be transformed.

How Vishvambhar Met Nityananda

Early each morning the Vaishnavas of Navadvip met along the riverbank. There they took their baths in the holy Ganges and prayed together. To their delight, Vishvambhar started to join them. He washed and dried their clothes, fetched sandalwood and flowers for their worship, and made himself useful in any way he could. Later in the day, he visited them in their homes, always bringing with him a gift. His wish was to serve them, and although they hesitated to accept his service, they loved him for it. They knew that he was destined for greatness. For the time being, though, they welcomed him as a new member of their community and accepted his offerings of service.

Since he was now part of their community, they told him of their fear of persecution. They were worried that they had enemies among the caste *brahmanas*, whom the Muslim rulers accepted as leaders among the Hindus. These *brahmanas* resented the Vaishnavas, who, as opposed to the caste-conscious society already established in Navadvip and throughout much of India, favored a religion based on love, in which anyone could pray directly to Krishna and receive God's grace, without the need for the *brahmanas'* priestly ceremonies.

At any time, the *brahmanas* could complain to the Muslim magistrate, known as the Kazi, and provoke him to suppress the Vaishnavas, perhaps even imprison their leaders. When Vishvambhar heard of these potential injustices, he spoke out among the devotees: "Who are these people that criticize you? Whoever they are, you have no need to fear them. Krishna will always protect his devotees."

Vishvambhar gave the Vaishnavas his promise that he himself would protect them. Hearing this, they believed that as long as he was with them, they would be safe.

·······

ONE DAY, GADADHAR TOOK HIS FRIEND NIMAI on a walk across the fields to visit Advaita's house. Advaita Acharya was the acknowledged elder among the Vaishnavas, and Gadadhar wanted to show him how Nimai, now known as Vishvambhar, had changed. Gadadhar hoped that Advaita would confirm what they all now believed, namely that Vishvambhar was destined to be their savior.

For his part, Advaita had been wanting this opportunity. He had watched Nimai for years from a distance—ever since he had first noticed him as the younger brother of Vishvarup—hoping that Nimai would turn out to be Krishna's answer to his prayers.

Since his return from Gaya, Nimai had undergone a profound transformation. He had become introspective and thoughtful, a spiritually absorbed young man. He was now unusually tall, and his commanding height added to his extraordinary personal beauty. Along with this, his new modesty and calm assurance gave him a dignified and masterful manner. As soon as Advaita saw this effulgent figure approaching, he believed himself to be in Krishna's presence.

"You have come at last, my Lord," he said. "The Vaishnavas have been waiting for you a long time. Please stay and always inspire us to chant Krishna's name."

Advaita brought out the lamps and incense normally reserved for the worship of Vishnu and with them he offered an *arati* ceremony to honor Vishvambhar. He finished by falling at his feet and reciting a mantra in praise of Krishna.

"I offer my respects to Krishna, Lord of the *brahmanas*. He is the benefactor of the cows, the *brahmanas* and the whole world. My repeated obeisances unto Govinda [Krishna]."

Gadadhar saw that Advaita considered Vishvambhar to be his worshipful Lord and was ready to be his servant; he was embarrassed to see an elder show such veneration to his friend. Aware of Gadadhar's embarrassment, Advaita quietly advised the young man: "You will soon understand that this friend of yours is no ordinary person."

Hearing these words and witnessing Advaita's change of heart, Gadadhar silently vowed that from that day forward he would serve Vishvambhar in every way. Advaita decided that before publicly joining Vishvambhar he would move away from Navadvip to his house in Shantipur, some twenty miles away, where he would await Vishvambhar's summons.

The two young friends, Gadadhar and Vishvambhar, returned home and from then on they were inseparable. Whenever his friend was lost in ecstasy, Gadadhar protected him; when he trembled with emotion, Gadadhar held him; and when Vishvambhar fainted while chanting Krishna's name, Gadadhar was there to catch him from falling. Vishvambhar's mother always worried for her son's safety, too. She made a special request to Gadadhar: "Please stay near us, dear boy, and always look after my son."

········

DAY AND NIGHT VISHVAMBHAR CALLED upon the name of Krishna and cried tears of love. News of his transformation attracted more attention than ever to the Vaishnavas. The orthodox *brahmanas* now openly opposed them. Just as the Vaishnavas feared, some of the *brahmanas* complained to the Muslim authorities. Rumors spread that the Kazi, anticipating a rise of religious fervor among the Hindus, planned to arrest some of the devotees. Shrivas, in particular, as their principle organizer, was afraid for himself and his family.

Vishvambhar heard all of this and went to Shrivas's house. He found him worshipping Narasingha, the half-human, half-lion form of Vishnu who protects his devotees from harm. Vishvambhar stood before Shrivas and roared like a lion. Shrivas had never seen Vishvambhar like this. It seemed to him that he saw before him Vishvambhar transformed into Narasingha. Shrivas trembled with fear, but then Vishvambhar spoke to him: "Don't you know yet who I am, Shrivas? I am the same Narasingha you have always worshipped. I have heard your prayers and come to protect you." Shrivas was stunned and at the same time filled with ecstasy. He prayed to Vishvambhar.

"O Lord, I did not recognize you. Disguised as an ordinary person you washed my clothes and served me, and so you bewildered me. Now I realize that you are Vishnu, you are Krishna, and you are Narasingha. My fear is gone."

Vishvambhar told him to bring the rest of his family so that they could also see him as Narasingha. Shrivas called his wife and children and his household to witness this wonder. They brought the articles of worship from their household altar and used them to worship Vishvambhar as Narasingha. He accepted their worship and assured them that, at any moment, he could change the hearts of the Kazi or any of his subjects, so they need not be afraid.

"In case you don't believe me, I will show you my powers," said Vishvambhar. He looked into the eyes of Shrivas's four-year-old niece Narayani and commanded her, "Chant Krishna's name, Narayani, and weep in ecstasy."

To everyone's amazement the little girl started to sing Krishna's names, and as she did so, she began to laugh and cry. From that day she was devoted to Vishvambhar, and Shrivas and his household never feared the King again.

·······

VISHVAMBHAR HAD NOW ESTABLISHED DEVOTION to Krishna as the theme of his life. He had found Advaita as his mentor; he had his intimate friend, Gadadhar; and his trusted helper, Shrivas. He spent his days surrounded by his friends, chanting and hearing about Krishna, and being overwhelmed with love for him. Yet there remained one close companion he would need to find before embarking upon his life's mission.

Nityananda was from East Bengal, born in the village of Ekachakra. From childhood he was a unique and inspiring personality, adored by everyone. He led his friends in endless playful reenacting of the lives of Krishna and Rama. This play so absorbed them day and night that they forgot even to go home to eat. One day, when Nityananda was twelve years old, a *sannyasi* stayed at his house and sat up through the night speaking with his father about Krishna, creating a deep impression on his devout host. In the morning when the *sannyasi* was ready to leave, he made a momentous request.

"Please allow your son to be my traveling companion," asked the holy man. "He is a special child and I will train him to be a great teacher."

Nityananda's father and mother were stunned by this proposal, but for the sake of their son's future they reluctantly agreed. So they parted with their beloved son who was their life and soul. Shortly afterward, his father died of a broken heart.[10]

Nityananda followed his new master as he traveled from place to place, serving him and learning from him to practice yoga and recite the scriptures. When he reached manhood, he took leave of his teacher and went on alone. Filled with love for Krishna, he traveled for twenty years in perpetual pilgrimage around the holy places of India.

On his journeys, Nityananda met the great mystic Madhavendra Puri, who was an ecstatic Vaishnava always absorbed in love of God. The two embraced and spoke for a long time. While speaking, they were frequently overcome with spiritual emotion to the point of tears, and Nityananda recognized Madhavendra to be his spiritual master. Madhavendra had other disciples, among them Advaita Acharya and Vishvambhar's guru, Ishvara Puri. This was how Nityananda became spiritually related to Vishvambhar and the Vaishnavas of Navadvip.

Having found his guru and having heard from him about Krishna, Nityananda went to Vrindavan, Krishna's original home. There he stayed, waiting for divine guidance to show him his destiny. One day, he heard that in Navadvip a great Vaishnava saint had arisen, who was chanting the names of Krishna and inspiring the whole region. He knew he must meet this saint. So Nityananda made his way to Navadvip, where a *brahmana* gave him shelter in his house.

·· ······

Vishvambhar awoke from an unusual dream and told his friends what he had seen: "I saw a majestic figure who reminded me of Krishna's brother, Balaram. This figure stood outside my house calling my name. I believe someone special has come to Navadvip to see me and we must find him."

His friends spent the morning looking for this wonderful person, but they returned without success. Vishvambhar decided that he would find the stranger himself, and in the afternoon he went out with them. He led them straight to the door of the house where Nityananda was staying. Inside, they beheld a handsome man dressed in white cloth with his hair drawn into a top-knot. It was Nityananda. Unaware of his visitors, he sat in deep meditation. They could all tell he was a great soul and they bowed before him. Then Vishvambhar stood directly in front of him and waited.

Nityananda opened his eyes to see the very person he had been seeking for so long. He was stunned with the recognition and could not speak. Prompted by Vishvambhar, one of the devotees recited a verse about Krishna. When he heard Krishna being described, Nityananda shuddered and rolled upon the floor in floods of tears. Vishvambhar raised him and the two embraced, floating in an ocean of love.

For a long time they held each other, crying with joy. Then Nityananda told of his endless pilgrimage; how wherever he went he saw only the holy place, but never Krishna; how he had searched everywhere for Krishna all his life; and now he had found him in Vishvambhar. The devotees looked on in wonder. They felt like they were seeing Rama and his brother, Lakshman, or the brothers Krishna and Balaram. After that, Nityananda stayed as a guest in Shrivas's house, and was counted as Vishvambhar's closest associate.

Vishvambhar's Mission

At home with her son and daughter-in-law, Sachi saw many unusual things. One day, Vishvambhar brought Nityananda home for lunch, and while Sachi watched the two friends eating together, before her eyes they were transformed into five-year-old boys, looking just like the brothers Krishna and Balaram. When she saw this, Sachi fainted and Vishvambhar had to run over to pick her up. He helped her to her room and there she wept and trembled, overcome by what she had seen. This was how she first began to suspect the divine identities of her son and Nityananda.

Each night the two could be seen together at Shrivas's house, where they journeyed deep into the ocean of spiritual love, singing and dancing with the devotees. In these ecstatic dances, Nityananda lost all inhibition and any sense of where he was or what he was doing, while all who took part shared in his joy.

Day and night Vishvambhar danced in the midst of the devotees at Shrivas's house. On occasion, he showed himself as the Supreme Being and displayed mystical powers accompanied by miraculous visions. When this happened, the devotees were frightened and asked him to stop. Then his mood would change as he became a humble devotee once again, weeping for Krishna and embracing his friends, begging them to help him see Krishna.

One day, Murari Gupta came to see Vishvambhar. As an old friend he offered his respects, first to Vishvambhar and then to Nityananda. Vishvambhar told him that he had made a mistake.

"Go home," he said, "and I will teach you something."

Murari went home and slept. In his dream he saw Nityananda walking in front of Vishvambhar. Then he saw Nityananda change into Balaram, carrying a plough and club, while Vishvambhar transformed into Krishna with a peacock feather in his hair. When Murari awoke, he remembered what Vishvambhar had said earlier. He realized the dream was showing him that Nityananda was the same as Balaram, Krishna's elder brother, and that Vishvambhar was the same as Krishna. Balaram always protected Krishna and, being senior to him, was therefore honored first. So he returned to Vishvambhar and this time offered his respects first to Nityananda then to Vishvambhar.

"Now you have understood," said Vishvambhar, pleased with his friend.

"Anyone who wishes to be my devotee should first venerate Nityananda. If you do that you will be dear to me."[11]

Vishvambhar had special love for Murari and later revealed to him that in a previous birth he had been Hanuman, servant of Rama.

Another devotee who came regularly to Shrivas's house was Shuklambar, a simple soul who lived in Navadvip and was loved by all the Vaishnavas. He devoted his time to chanting Krishna's names. To keep body and soul together he begged alms from nearby houses by collecting broken rice in a small bag. Broken rice was of poor quality, but it was his only food. One day Vishvambhar seized a handful of this rice and ate it, exactly as Krishna had once eaten the rice brought to him in Dvaraka by his childhood friend Sudama. Vishvambhar chewed the morsels of rice with relish. When Shuklambar protested that such broken rice was not fit for him to eat, Vishvambhar laughed and taught everyone present.

"Chanting Krishna's names is all you need for success in this age. The name is the incarnation of Krishna and by chanting this name you are directly in his presence. No other method—either study or penance or good works— is necessary for salvation. Be like Shuklambar, patient and humble, and be like the tree that neither protests nor asks for favors. Simply accept whatever comes as the grace of God. In this mood, you will be able to chant Krishna's names constantly."

One hot day, after dancing and singing together for a long time, the devotees were exhausted. Vishvambhar planted a mango seed in the dry earth, and before everyone's eyes it grew into a mature tree bearing ripe mangoes. From this tree, Vishvambhar collected about two hundred fruits, each of them juicy and without a seed, and fed them to all present. The tree miraculously lived on to produce fruits daily throughout the year.

········

VISHVAMBHAR DECIDED that the time had come to bring Advaita Acharya closer and include him in the mystic assemblies each night at Shrivas's house, so he sent word for him to come. Advaita had so far seen Vishvambhar in the role of a devotee, but what he really wanted was to see Vishvambhar show his divine majesty. Vishvambhar knew this, so on the day Advaita came to see him, Vishvambhar manifested a transformation in himself and his companions.

When Advaita arrived at Shrivas's house, he found Vishvambhar sitting on a throne in the center of his devotees. Nityananda held an umbrella over his head, Gadadhar served him on one side and Shrivas on the other. Advaita saw the scene as a heavenly vision. Instead of seeing Vishvambhar in the company of his friends, he saw him transformed into Vishnu, worshipped by gods like Brahma and Shiva. In ecstasy, Advaita, along with his wife, Sita, fell at Vishvambhar's feet. Vishvambhar placed those divine feet on Advaita's head as a gesture of humility. Advaita's dream was fulfilled and at that moment he surrendered himself fully to the service of Vishvambhar.

"I have come to teach everyone to be loving servants of Krishna," said Vishvambhar. "In every town and village I will spread my movement of love for God." Hearing these words, Advaita added his own special request: "Please, Lord, when you preach, do not forget the less fortunate souls—the poor, the downtrodden, the fallen, and the foolish. Include them all in your mercy."

"It doesn't matter who they are, they shall be included," vowed Vishvambhar. "Only those who are too proud to accept my help will escape. Even if they appear to be religious, if they are proud I cannot help them."

The nightly chanting sessions continued, now including Advaita, and the number of chanters grew. Vishvambhar welcomed them all, embracing each newcomer as an old friend. Each one found in him the divine person they were looking for—some as the magnificent Vishnu, some as lordly Rama, and some as gentle Krishna. At the same time, they saw him as a humble servant of Krishna who prayed and wept in the mood of a devotee.

Sachi also came to the chanting sessions. She watched her son transported by his ecstasies, his hair and clothing in disarray as he fell to the ground and rolled in the dust, and she feared he would hurt himself. Since she could not prevent him, she could only pray to Krishna that he would not come to any harm, and that she would always be with him, absorbed in singing Krishna's holy names.

The Great Revelation

During their nightlong chanting at Shrivas's house, the devotees felt time stand still, as if a single night lasted for eternity. Sometimes the chanters caught a glimpse of Vishvambhar's divine nature, when for a few moments he showed his magnificence. Usually he was wrapped in a mood of devotion, in love with Krishna. However, there was one particular occasion when, without reservation, he showed his divine nature.

On this day, he stood up to dance as usual, then approached Shrivas's household shrine and sat down on the altar in the place meant for Vishnu. Before everyone's eyes he changed into a dazzling divine personality. All present could understand they were in the presence of Vishnu himself; they felt as if the shadows of illusion fell away and they saw Vishvambhar for the first time as he truly was, as the Supreme Lord. So began what they later called the Great Revelation, a mystical transformation that lasted for twenty-one hours.

In awe, wishing to honor the divine person before them, the devotees worshipped him. They began by bathing Vishvambhar with pots of Ganges water, scented with herbs and oils. Nityananda was the first to pour water over Vishvambhar's head, and then each took their turn, even the servants and children, so that everyone had the chance to offer homage.

After bathing Vishvambhar, they dressed him in fresh garments and massaged his feet with fragrant oils. They brought him offerings of fruits and flowers and performed the *arati* ceremony to Vishnu. Next they wanted to feed him. Running here and there, they gathered the best foods from wherever they could, collecting fruits, sweets, and dairy products to prepare wonderful dishes for their Lord.

As he ate, Vishvambhar described the lives of some of those present, speaking of events known only to each of them. He reminded Shrivas of the time he had attended a lecture on the *Srimad Bhagavatam* and been overwhelmed to hear about Krishna. Shrivas had broken down in tears; his fellow students, not understanding what was wrong, had carried him outside and left him lying on the ground; Shrivas, feeling hurt and misunderstood, had gone home and read the *Srimad Bhagavatam* again and again, his eyes still filled with tears.

"I saw your unhappiness and entered your heart, filling you with love," he told Shrivas. "That is why you always feel such bliss when you hear the *Bhagavatam*."

Then he turned to Gangadas, his former teacher.

"Do you remember when, afraid of persecution by the Kazi, you set out with your family at night to escape from his soldiers and cross the Ganges? You could not find a boat, and as dawn approached you stood on the bank shaking with fear. You were at the point of throwing yourselves into the river when I came as a ferryman to rescue you. It was I who saved you all and carried you across the Ganges." Hearing this, Gangadas fainted.

Next, Vishvambhar remembered his old friend Shridhar, the banana seller, who he used to provoke so mischievously when he was younger.

"Go to the bank of the Ganges," he told the devotees, "and listen for someone calling upon the name of Krishna. Bring that person to me."

Some of them went in the direction of the Ganges and there they heard a voice in the darkness. It was Shridhar. At the end of each day, having sold his bananas in the market, Shridhar spent the night in prayer, repeating Krishna's name beside the flowing waters. They brought him to the house and into the midst of the gathering. Shridhar came face to face with the same Nimai who used to joke with him at his banana stall. When he saw Nimai transformed into a divine being, Shridhar almost fainted.

"Shridhar, you always call my name," said Vishvambhar, "So now I have called your name and brought you here. You served me well, giving me everything I asked even without being paid, and you let me trick you many times. Now I want to give you any boon you care to ask. But first I give you the eyes to see me as I am."

Before his eyes, Shridhar saw Vishvambhar transformed into Krishna playing his flute.

"Come, you can have a whole planet if you wish. Just ask me."

Shridhar hesitated, his eyes fixed upon Krishna's feet.

"All I want is that you be my master, and let me sing your name."

"Then I bless you with pure devotional service. That is the greatest gift I can give," declared Vishvambhar. Shridhar wept with joy and everyone sang Krishna's names.

Vishvambhar was especially fond of Haridas Thakur, who had borne great suffering for the sake of his devotion to Krishna. Haridas had been raised a Muslim, but at an early age found faith in Krishna and a great attachment to chanting Krishna's names. Long ago, after Haridas had become a devotee of Hari, he had been brought before the king to be punished for chanting Krishna's name. Haridas fearlessly told the king that the *Qur`an* and the *Puranas* both describe the same God.

"All the people of the world worship the same God, according to their natures and the scriptures God has given them," Haridas said.

But the king was hard-hearted and had Haridas beaten in twenty-two market places, then thrown in the Ganges and left for dead. Miraculously, Haridas was washed ashore unharmed, and later he was taken in and befriended by Advaita Acharya. All this had happened before Vishvambhar was born. Haridas had prayed with Advaita, and together they had implored the Supreme Lord to descend into this world and rescue people from their ignorance and suffering.

"My heart broke when you were beaten, Haridas," Vishvambhar said. "You felt no anger against your attackers and on account of your love I could not harm them. I myself took the blows from your back so that you felt no pain.[12] I am your servant. For your sake I am here. I will do anything for you."

Haridas prayed to Vishvambhar to always be able to serve the Vaishnavas, and Vishvambhar blessed him that he would forever love and serve Krishna and his devotees. Haridas's ceaseless chanting of Krishna's names made him the example for all Vaishnavas to follow.

"What of Mukunda, Lord, what benediction will you give him?" Shrivas asked, but Vishvambhar had no blessing for Mukunda.

Mukunda had a beautiful voice and Vishvambhar had always loved to hear him sing. They had been together since Mukunda enrolled as one of the first pupils in Nimai's Sanskrit academy. However, Vishvambhar had become unhappy with Mukunda, because he mixed with teachers opposed to devotional service to Krishna. For this reason, Vishvambhar had barred him from their gatherings. But Mukunda was unable to stay away; that very night he was in the room, hiding behind a curtain.

Hearing from his hiding place that Vishvambhar had nothing to say about him, the distraught Mukunda whispered to Shrivas, asking if he would ever be allowed to see Vishvambhar again? Shrivas went to Vishvambhar and made a plea on Mukunda's behalf.

"After ten million births he will see me," responded Vishvambhar, "This is certain."

"I will, I will!" came Mukunda's involuntary cry from behind the curtain.

Vishvambhar, laughing, called him out. Weeping with relief and happiness, he was brought before his master.

"My blessing to you is that I will spread my love through your voice. Wherever I am, you will be there as my singer, and when my devotees hear your voice their hearts will melt."

"Haribol, Haribol!" cried the devotees, and Mukunda once more began to sing for Vishvambhar.

· · • • • • • · ·

Crowds of well-wishers brought gifts to honor Sachi and her newborn child (see page 15).

Little Nimai ran about the house, playing with his older brother Vishvarup and delighting his parents as they watched their son's energetic explorations (see page 17).

When Nimai was frustrated, someone would start to chant Krishna's names.
Then Nimai was happy again (see page 20).

Nimai was devoted to his older brother, Vishvarup, whose gentle nature made
him loved and respected by all (see page 22).

Nimai was given the sacred thread and enrolled as a student of the learned teacher, Gangadas Pandit (see page 24).

Nimai and Lakshmidevi possessed such an aura of beauty and grace that people thought they were witnessing Vishnu and his eternal consort the goddess Lakshmi herself (see page 29).

Nimai taught his students on the bank of the Ganges, sitting like the moon surrounded by stars. He would first prove a point, then disprove it, then prove it again. No other pandit could match him (see page 32).

At Nimai's invitation, the champion scholar Digvijaya composed spontaneous poetry to entertain them all. For three hours he glorified the Ganges, chanting Sanskrit verses with ease (see page 33).

At his mother's request Nimai married a second time. The whole town came to celebrate his wedding to Vishnupriya, lavishly hosted by a wealthy citizen of Navadvipa (see page 37).

When Nimai gazed at Vishnu's footprint in Gaya, he was overcome by a flood of emotion. Tears filled his eyes, his body shivered, and he fell to the ground in a state of ecstasy (see page 43).

Nimai bowed before the devout teacher Ishvara Puri and asked him for the gift of Krishna's lotus feet (see page 44).

Ishvara Puri accepted Nimai as his disciple and gave him the sacred ten-syllabled mantra made up of names of Krishna (see page 44).

Nimai's mother and wife saw a change in his behavior. He only spoke of Krishna
and kept them awake at night with his tears, as he cried with spiritual longing for
Krishna, the Lord of his life (see page 47).

Nimai told his students he could no longer be their teacher. He told them that he
could only speak of Krishna and tied up his bundle of books (see page 49).

When Vishvambhar met Nityananda, the two embraced, floating in an ocean of love, and for a long time they held each other, crying with joy (see page 54).

Vishvambhar sat on the altar in the place meant for Vishnu. Before everyone's eyes he changed into a dazzling divine personality. So began what they later called the Great Revelation, a mystical transformation that lasted for twenty-one hours (see page 58).

EACH EVENING WHEN THE CHANTING BEGAN at Shrivas's house, Vishvambhar wanted the doors closed to everyone except devotees, for there were many ready to disapprove of what they were doing, who might try to disrupt the meetings. On one occasion, Shrivas made an exception and allowed a monk to secretly watch the chanting. Vishvambhar danced and chanted as usual, but after some time he stopped.

"Why do I feel no ecstasy?" he asked. "It must be because an intruder is hiding here. Who is it?"

"It is a pure-hearted monk whom I secretly allowed in," admitted Shrivas.

Vishvambhar was displeased and sent the monk away. He left without complaint, simply thinking himself fortunate to have had just a glimpse of Vishvambhar's dancing. Understanding his heart, Vishvambhar called him back to openly join in.

Despite the devotees' caution, rumors circulated about what went on behind their closed doors. One night, a *brahmana* named Gopal Chapala left a large flagon of wine outside the house in full view of passersby. He did this to discredit Shrivas, to make it look as if instead of chanting they were drinking.

Tongues began to wag. Some said Shrivas would ruin the reputation of the neighborhood. A campaign started against Vishvambhar and the Vaishnavas, led by some of the influential *brahmanas* of Navadvip. They worried for their livelihoods as priests, but most of all they feared Vishvambhar would unsettle the Muslim rulers. As it turned out, their fears were well founded. Word had already reached the Muslim king that a religious revival was stirring in Navadvip, and in high places questions were being asked. Vishvambhar, however, was fearless.

Saving the Fallen

Vishvambhar wanted to start a popular movement based on *sankirtan*, community chanting of God's names. So he sent out his two most experienced and trusted companions, Nityananda and Haridas, to beseech people to chant the name of Krishna. Each day the two of them visited many homes with a simple request: "Please chant Krishna's name, worship Krishna, and teach others about Krishna."

Most people were happy to hear this message, but some resisted such a direct appeal. Undeterred by any resistance they encountered, Nityananda and Haridas continued. One day they came upon two drunkards fighting in the street, brothers known as Jagai and Madhai. Despite having been raised in a good family, they were thieves and murderers who terrorized the people of Navadvip. Passersby warned Nityananda not to interfere with these men, who were feared even by officers of the law, but their warnings had the opposite effect on Nityananda. He thought that if these two infamous criminals could be rescued from their fallen condition, then everyone would give credit to Vishvambhar. Ignoring the warnings, Nityananda boldly approached them.

"Krishna is your father," he called loudly. "Chant Krishna's name, give up your sins, and worship Krishna!"

Stupefied by drink, Jagai and Madhai looked up in surprise to see who dared to accost them. They saw two Vaishnavas, people who represented everything they detested. Filled with rage they leaped at them, intent on doing grievous harm. Nityananda and Haridas ran for their lives, pursued by the drunken pair.

"Thanks to you we could get ourselves killed," shouted Haridas as they ran, but Nityananda only laughed. The thieves were fat and drunk and could not hope to catch the nimble devotees; all they could do was shout obscenities. Nityananda and Haridas safely reached Shrivas's house, and breathlessly told their master what had happened. Vishvambhar was pleased with their work and congratulated them.

Haridas, however, was worried that his partner would try again and this time endanger them all, so he complained to Advaita Acharya about Nityananda's wild ways, and asked him to talk some sense into him. Advaita, however, assured Haridas that very soon he would see those two ruffians saved by Nityananda and Vishvambhar. Hearing this, Haridas resigned himself to whatever might follow.

Jagai and Madhai continued their drunken ways. Yet they were drawn by the sound of singing and musical instruments coming from Shrivas's house. They frequented the area just to hear it. In their drunken state they danced to the music and joined in the singing, unaware of its spiritual potency. Sometimes they saw Vishvambhar pass by and shouted after him.

"Nimai Pandit," they called out. "We like your music! We will visit you and bring you gifts as well."

Vishvambhar took no notice, but one evening Nityananda again met them in the street. Madhai became angry and without warning attacked Nityananda, striking him a severe blow on his forehead with a broken piece of pot. Nityananda was badly cut and the wound began to bleed. At this, Jagai was remorseful, because even he feared the consequences of harming a holy man like Nityananda. He caught hold of his brother to restrain him and the two were locked in a struggle. Nityananda, although his forehead was bleeding, was unafraid. He stood his ground, determined not to give up on these two misguided souls.

News was carried swiftly to Vishvambhar, who quickly appeared on the spot. He drew himself up to his full height and manifested in his hand the divine *chakra* of Vishnu, a razor-sharp weapon meant to cut off the heads of demons. Vishvambhar was ready to use it in defense of Nityananda. Seeing him towering over them like death personified, with a blazing disc spinning in his outstetched hand, the wretched brothers were paralyzed with fear. At that moment, Nityananda intervened.

"Do not kill them," he said. "These two are mine. I have forgiven them and I want them spared. Please be peaceful and give them to me. Though Madhai attacked me, his brother Jagai tried to stop him." When Vishvambhar heard that Jagai had tried to hold back his brother, he softened toward him.

"You tried to protect my Nityananda, so from this day I give you pure love for Krishna." With these words Vishvambhar embraced Jagai, who tearfully fell to the ground. Jagai and Madhai's hearts beat as one, for they did everything together. No sooner had Jagai's heart changed than Madhai's also changed, and he too fell at Vishvambhar's feet, begging forgiveness.

"You injured the body of my beloved Nityananda, so I cannot forgive you," said Vishvambhar to Madhai. "Only if you fall before him and hold on to his feet can you be saved." Hearing this, Madhai fell at Nityananda's feet and begged his forgiveness. Nityananda had no need to forgive him, since he had not accepted his offense in the first place. He turned to Vishvambhar: "Lord, you have the power to show your mercy to Madhai. Whatever good deeds I have done I give them to him. Now you please save him."

"Then you must embrace him," said Vishvambhar, "and by your touch he will be saved." Nityananda took Madhai in his arms and held him tight. As he did so, Madhai was infused with pure love. The two brothers, by now completely subdued, prayed before Vishvambhar and surrendered themselves to him.

"Sin no more. All your past sins are washed away," he said, then ordered his companions, "Take these two to my house. Tonight I will chant with them and make them the best of devotees."

That evening the *kirtan* was more intense than usual. Before long, Jagai and Madhai were dancing with the devotees, and in the dance both of them were touched by Vishvambhar. At the end, they fell before each one of the devotees and received their blessings. Vishvambhar made a declaration: "From now on I personally live in the bodies of Jagai and Madhai, and whoever serves them serves me."

Vishvambhar's followers saw the astonishing transformation in these two sinful men as the proof of the power of his love. But Vishvambhar said it was all due to Nityananda's mercy.

••••••••

ONE DAY, NITYANANDA WAS WANDERING carefree in the streets of Navadvip when Madhai appeared before him. Falling at his feet, Madhai washed them with his tears.

"Please forgive this ungrateful soul for the harm he caused you," he prayed.

"Rise Madhai, you are mine and I am yours," said Nityananda. "Does a father take offense from his infant son? You have received my master's mercy. Therefore, there is no fault in you."

"Master, I am troubled by one thing. I grievously hurt countless people in Navadvip. I do not even know who they are, so I cannot beg their forgiveness. How can I make amends?"

"Build a bathing *ghat* beside the Ganges," Nityananda instructed him, "Greet each one who comes to bathe in her sacred waters, and humbly beg their forgiveness."

So Madhai, his heart heavy with remorse, leveled a platform beside the Ganges and dug steps to serve as a bathing place. There he stayed, spade in hand to maintain the place, daily from dawn to dusk. Chanting the names of Krishna, he served all who came to bathe and cared for their clothes.

"Forgive whatever offenses I have made against you," he begged each one with folded hands. "Please show your mercy to this fallen soul."

When the townspeople saw the change in Madhai and his brother, Jagai, they were deeply moved.

"Nimai Pandit is no ordinary person," they said. "Truly he has divine power to be able to change the hearts of two such as these." And from that day none of the townspeople of Navadvip spoke ill of Vishvambhar, the savior of Jagai and Madhai.

Conversion of the Kazi

The people of Navadvip had heard of the nightly gatherings at Shrivas's house, and they longed to be allowed to witness them. They knew that because of the disapproval of their own orthodox leaders, as well as their Muslim overlords, the *kirtans* were not open to everyone. They longed for the day when Vishvambhar would let them witness the miraculous chanting that had so transformed the hearts of Jagai and Madhai. Soon their wishes were fulfilled.

As more and more homes heeded the requests of Vishvambhar's devotees, the sounds of drums and cymbals were heard in the evenings from houses across town. Daily, people visited Vishvambhar and begged him to come out and chant publicly among them. He asked them to faithfully chant Krishna's names, and taught them the Maha-mantra, the great chant for deliverance:

Hare Krishna Hare Krishna
Krishna Krishna Hare Hare
Hare Rama Hare Rama
Rama Rama Hare Hare

He taught them to chant these names at any time or place, either as *japa*, praying softly to themselves, or as *sankirtan*, singing together with their family and friends.

As a result of these instructions people began to chant Krishna's names regularly. Each day at sunset they would gather in their homes to sing, and their melodious chanting spread from village to village throughout the district.

But unease also spread through the community as some muttered disapproval, and others, perceiving the chanting as a threat to the established order, complained to their Muslim rulers. One day, the Kazi walked through the town and heard for himself the sound of *sankirtan* coming from many houses. His response was to send armed guards into several homes, including Shrivas's house, to seize the drums and break them. Some devotees were arrested and beaten, while others fled.

"From now on, *sankirtan* is banned," ordered the Kazi. "Today I am excusing you, but if I find anyone doing this in the future, I will seize their property and forcibly convert them to Islam."

The devotees were afraid. They brought the news to Vishvambhar, but he was defiant: "Continue your *sankirtan* and do not fear. I will protect you from the Muslims." Despite hearing these words from Vishvambhar, people were still afraid of the Kazi. But even the fear of being arrested could not prevent them from chanting. By this chanting they called down Krishna's mercy.

Vishvambhar decided it was time for public action. He sent out word calling all the townspeople to gather for a huge demonstration in the form of a *sankirtan* procession that very evening. He wanted a great festival, and asked people to decorate the roads and organize themselves in each of the nine districts of Navadvip.

"Bring torches from every home," he said. "Bring your musical instruments. We will have *sankirtan* and see if this Kazi can stop us!"

The townships buzzed with excitement. At last they were to witness Vishvambhar's ecstatic dancing. For one year they had waited, hearing only rumors of events in Shrivas's house, and their eagerness to join his movement had grown to a deep longing. While men busied themselves preparing torches and gathering musical instruments, women decorated the houses with lamps and waterpots, coconuts and banana trees, and artistic patterns on the road outside the threshold of each doorway. As evening approached, Vishvambhar formed three *sankirtan* groups. One group was led by Haridas; a second was led by Advaita and Shrivas; and a third was led by Vishvambhar, with Nityananda and Gadadhar dancing on either side of him. Thus for the first time Vishvambhar came out to perform his chanting and dancing for everyone to witness.

As the setting sun tinged the sky with pink rays, Vishvambhar and his three groups of chanters emerged from Shrivas's house and passed through each of the quarters of Navadvip. Vishvambhar danced along the shore of the Ganges, past his childhood playground where he first met Lakshmidevi, past the place where as Nimai Pandit he had taught his students, past Madhai's *ghat*, through the main square of the town where he had discoursed into the night, moving steadily toward the Kazi's palace. Around him gathered a huge and highly charged procession, all seeking a glimpse of their inspiring leader.

Beautiful Vishvambhar, his golden features shining, danced in their midst. His tall frame swayed with arms extended like golden pillars to the sky. His strong shoulders and broad chest were encircled with a garland of jasmine flowers reaching to his knees. Dark curling hair framed his moonlike face, where tears rolled like pearls down his glowing cheeks. As he danced, he sang the names of Krishna and smiled, and his body, rapt in ecstasy, trembled like a *kadamba* flower caught in the wind. Watching his every move, the chanters were transfixed, unable to take their eyes from his godlike form.

Lit by thousands of torches, the night sky reverberated with the sound of massed drums and cymbals, as a flood of impassioned devotees converged upon the Kazi's home, surging through his grounds, trampling his flower gardens and starting fires. His guards fled, offering no resistance, leaving the Kazi undefended. Fearing for his life, he hid in his private quarters. Vishvambhar saw the wild state of the crowd and calmed them. Entering the inner courtyard, he sat down outside the Kazi's door and sent a respected citizen inside to persuade the Kazi to come out. The Muslim ruler eventually emerged, shaking with fear. Vishvambhar assured him that he was safe and respectfully offered him a seat.

·······

IT HAPPENED THAT VISHVAMBHAR'S GRANDFATHER-IN-LAW, Nilambara Chakravarti, had been almost an uncle to the Kazi when he was young. Vishvambhar recalled this relationship by calling the governor uncle, and again promised no harm would befall him. The governor composed himself and exchanged words with Vishvambhar. For some time they debated the relative merits of Hindu and Muslim scriptures, after which Vishvambhar put a question to the Kazi: "Lately you have not interfered with us, even when we have chanted openly. And tonight we have brought our drums and cymbals right to your doorstep without hindrance. Why have you not tried to stop us?"

"I have been afraid," admitted the Kazi. "The night I ordered your drums to be broken I dreamt a terrifying lion-headed creature sprang upon my chest and threatened me. See the marks of his claws." Here he opened his shirt and showed the marks of a lion's claws on his chest. "He demanded that I stop persecuting you for chanting the names of Krishna and Hari, or he would kill me. The next day, several of my men told me their faces had been burned and their beards singed by flames when they had come near your devotees to stop them from chanting. All these things have frightened me, so I have decided to leave you alone." With tears in his eyes, the Kazi lowered his voice. "In my heart, I feel you to be the divine Vishnu whom the Hindus worship."

"You have spoken the names of Krishna, Hari, and Vishnu," said Vishvambhar. "Therefore you are now freed from all sins." When he heard this, the Kazi bent down and touched Vishvambhar's feet, begging for his mercy. Then he spoke in a loud voice.

"From this day on," the Kazi declared, "no descendant of mine shall hinder the *sankirtan* movement. This is my order." When the crowd heard this, they cheered, "Hari! Hari!" and Vishvambhar led them again in ecstatic chanting of the holy names. No more damage was done to the governor's property, and order was restored. The Kazi safely reentered his home, and the crowds, after much chanting and jubilation, went peacefully to their beds. All those citizens of Navadvip who saw Vishvambhar's ecstatic dancing on this night and witnessed these events felt their lives had been blessed beyond measure.

Truth from a Child

After the Kazi's proclamation, Vishvambhar started to go out daily along the roads of Navadvip. He took with him singers, dancers, and musicians with drums and cymbals. Their beautiful processions captured the hearts of the people and many became Vaishnavas.

A devotee composed a song of Vishvambhar's *sankirtan*:

When the sun rose in the east
The golden Lord went out
Through the towns and villages
With singers all about

Tathai, tathai, called the drum
The cymbals chimed in time
His ankle-bells danced, his golden form
Trembled with love divine

Mukunda, Madhava, Yadava, Hari
Filled every chanter's mouth
They woke the people from their dreams
By singing words of truth

For human life you do not care
This gift so precious and high
Your love with Krishna you don't share
And so your days drift by

Life is short and quickly gone
Filled with sorrow and pain
Leave aside your hopes and fears
And sing the holy name

Each time the sun arises and sets
Another day is through
Why stay idle, when you can serve
The Lord who dwells with you?

Taste the sweetness of Krishna's name
Which rises like the sun
It fills the world with purest light
And blesses everyone

·······

ONE NIGHT SOON AFTER THE GREAT PUBLIC PROCESSION, Vishvambhar was at Shrivas's house, absorbed in singing with his friends. Shrivas's young son had been unwell and was being nursed in another room. Soon, cries of distress were heard. Shrivas went to see what was the matter and found his family in deep shock. They told him his son had died. He sat with his distressed family crowded around the boy's bed. Shrivas accepted the child's death as the will of the Lord. He did not want grief to spoil Vishvambhar's chanting, so without informing his guests of his terrible loss he stayed quietly with his grieving family and comforted them. He did his best to reassure his wife that after all, this was a most fortunate way for their child's soul to leave this world, in the presence of Vishvambhar and so many exalted souls, while hearing the singing of the names of God.

"My son has achieved life's greatest goal, to pass away hearing Krishna's name," he said. "He is certainly liberated from birth and death and even now he is in the spiritual world." He appealed to his family to hold their grief in their hearts and not show their emotion until after Vishvambhar and the devotees had left. His words restrained them somewhat, as, in silence, they prepared the child's body for his last rites.

Saying nothing of his bereavement, Shrivas returned to the chanting, where he sang with more intensity than usual. After some time, Vishvambhar stopped the *kirtan*.

"Shrivas, I am feeling unhappy. What sorrow has entered this house?"

"In your presence, master, there can be no sorrow," said Shrivas.

Vishvambhar was not convinced. When he learned what happened, he became very grave. Realizing that Shrivas had not wanted to disturb him with the news, he thought how much his friends loved him, and how, for his sake, they would not even grieve for their own children. He wondered how he would ever be able to leave the company of those who loved him so dearly. He began to weep. Those near him heard him talk of leaving, but none knew what this could possibly mean.

Vishvambhar went to see the boy. With the entire household gathered around, he took the dead boy's hand in his and spoke gently to him.

"Why did you leave your father's house?"

To everyone's astonishment, the boy opened his eyes and replied, "Who is father and who is son? My karma brought me to this body and now it is time for me to leave and enter another one. You, Lord, control my destiny and I move according to your will, with no power to resist. My stay in Shrivas's home has been my great fortune, and I beg forgiveness for my offenses at his feet. Now, dear Lord of my heart, please allow me to leave and bless me that I may never forget you."

All heard the boy speak and watched him fall silent, his body lifeless once more. Hearing these words of truth, Shrivas and his relatives were enlightened and their grief was washed away. They touched Vishvambhar's feet, drowning their sorrows in tears of love and acceptance.

Vishvambhar personally carried the child's body to the Ganges, followed by Shrivas and his brothers. There they performed the last rites and burned the body to ashes. They scattered those ashes with chants of "Hari!" into the ever-flowing waters of Mother Ganges, who has borne the tears and laughter of all who live upon her banks since time immemorial. Then Vishvambhar made a promise.

"Dear Shrivas, you have lost your earthly son, but because of your loving care for me and my brother Nityananda, we will remain bound to you eternally as your spiritual sons."

········

A MAID WORKED IN SHRIVAS'S HOUSE. Her name was Duhkhi, which means "unhappy." She labored hard to keep the house clean and to serve the family in numerous ways. Each night she witnessed Vishvambhar's chanting, and she was present during his Great Revelation, when she had the chance to offer service to him along with the family.

Each evening Duhkhi collected water from the Ganges, carrying many waterpots on her head. While coming and going she caught glimpses of Vishvambhar's secret dancing. Back and forth she toiled, until a row of waterpots stood as testament to her labors, ready for the devotees to refresh themselves. One night, Vishvambhar considered the waterpots standing all around him, each filled to the brim with Ganges water, and asked Shrivas who it was that worked so hard to fill them. Shrivas told him that it was his servant, Duhkhi.

"Duhkhi is not the name for such a faithful servant. In my heart she will always be Sukhi," declared Vishvambhar. *Sukhi* means "happy." From that night, everyone called her by her new name, and Shrivas never again thought of her as his servant.

Renouncing the World

In the days that followed, Vishvambhar passed from one state of inner ectsasy to another. Sometimes he was lost in the mood of Rama, sometimes Krishna, sometimes Narasimha. Each of the great avatars of Vishnu was revealed in him at different times. Sometimes, thinking himself Balaram, he laughed and danced wildly, calling for honey and wine. At such times, only Nityananda could restrain him.

Increasingly, he became absorbed in the emotions of the *gopis*, the cowherd girls of Vrindavan forest who loved Krishna more than life itself. They had joined Krishna in the mystic circle of his Rasa dance, called the *rasamandala*, and their love for him was the supreme expression of self-surrender. When Krishna left Vrindavan, the *gopis* felt the pain of separation to be almost unbearable. Now Vishvambhar's heart was filled with this same undying love experienced by the *gopis*. Overwhelmed by these intense feelings, he wept openly in the company of his friends. His mother could not bear to see him like this, so she stayed at home and simply cried for her son.

A young *brahmana*, a former student of Vishvambhar, heard about his crying and was curious. People said Nimai Pandit had become a great saint and this student wanted to see for himself. One day he crept into Vishvambhar's house and found him calling loudly the names "*gopi*" and "Vrindavan."

For the student, versed by his former teacher in conventional religion, this behavior was strange and irrational. He interrupted Vishvambhar's trance, advising him to not call out the word *gopi*, but instead to chant the name of Krishna. Vishvambhar, filled with the feelings of a village girl who loved Krishna, and unaware who addressed him, cried out: "Krishna is a thief. What will I gain by chanting his name? Why should I worship Krishna, who abandoned us in Vrindavan so he could become a prince in Mathura?"

Saying this, Vishvambhar caught hold of a stick and chased away the young *brahmana*, who escaped only because some of Vishvambhar's friends intervened to save him.

The young man told his friends what had happened. They were caste *brahmanas* used to being honored by all, and when they heard his story they grew indignant. This Nimai Pandit, whom they once looked up to, had no respect for them and now was leading others astray. They thought Vishvambhar must be losing his mind, so they spread gossip against him and his followers. By doing this, they sowed the seeds of envy and doubt among their community.

Vishvambhar heard of this and was thoughtful. He did not want his new *sankirtan* movement to be threatened by lies and gossip, so he decided the time had come for him to enter the next stage of his life's mission. In a quiet place he spoke privately to Nityananda.

"Dear Nitai, I came to this world to save people from pain and illusion. But if they mock me as a sentimentalist everything will be spoiled, and they will have to continue suffering. Therefore I will give up family life and become a *sannyasi*. I will leave Navadvip, and my dear mother and wife, and travel as a mendicant, begging alms at people's doors; then everyone will respect me as a *sannyasi* and so they will be saved."[13] Nityananda heard this proposal in silence.

"Please give me your permission," Vishvambhar pleaded. "If you want people to take our chanting seriously, you must allow me to do this."

"I have no power to prevent you," replied Nityananda. "Whatever you decide you will do, and I will just have to trust that it will turn out to be right. But grant me one thing; before you take this step, tell your friends of your intentions and hear what they have to say."

Following this advice, Vishvambhar spoke first with Mukunda, whose singing he loved to hear. From childhood they had been very close, and Mukunda's gentle nature made him a source of good advice. When Mukunda saw Vishvambhar, he was happy, and sang him a beautiful song about

Krishna. Then Vishvambhar spoke of his intentions.

"I will shave my head and become a monk, Mukunda. Do not doubt me. I will do this and leave here to travel all over the world as a *sannyasi*."

Mukunda was distraught. He knew Vishvambhar could not be dissuaded. With sadness in his heart, he made one request.

"Please stay with us a little longer so that we can sing together a few more times, then do whatever you must do."

Next, Vishvambhar spoke with Gadadhar. Their friendship for each other was tender, for Gadadhar had always cared for him like a second brother. When Gadadhar heard the news, he was shocked.

"Why all of a sudden must you leave household life? Did anyone ever attain Krishna by shaving his head? What will become of your dear mother? Without you she will be all alone and will not be able to live. You will kill her! Just stay here and live as a householder, and together we will all serve Krishna. But if you are determined, then you must do as you please."

As Vishvambhar's intentions became known, everyone was distressed. Seeing their misery made him unhappy.

"I promise you that whatever happens we will never be separated," he assured them. "You are all my eternal companions. In life after life you will see me. Whenever I come to this world you will be with me. You will always find me in the bliss of *sankirtan,* and you will see me keeping my image in your homes." With such assurances he calmed their fears.

At last, Vishvambhar had to tell his mother. When she learned that her son would leave home, she could hardly breathe. Amid her tears she poured out her heart to him.

"O Nimai, please don't go. How will I live without seeing your beautiful moonlike face, your lotus eyes and long arms. You fill my house with light even without lamps. Your followers and friends are here—stay with them and have your *sankirtan* here in our house. Nitai will help you. If you abandon your mother, people will think you are hard-hearted, which is the opposite of your nature. How will you then teach them to love God?"

At first, Vishvambhar was silent. Then he spoke softly to give her courage.

"Listen, mother dear, and hear our secret. For many lifetimes you have been my mother. When I appeared as Vamana, you were my mother Aditi; as Devahuti you bore me as Kapila; you were Kaushalya and I your son Ramachandra; then you became Devaki and I was your son Krishna. Birth after birth, you are my mother; we can never be separated. This is the truth."

Sachi heard these words and was consoled, as if she had regained her life.

Having given everyone notice of his intentions, Vishvambhar abided by Mukunda's request and let matters rest for a while. He entered a last exuberant phase of sharing his love with his dear friends and followers in Navadvip. In the back of their minds they all knew his departure was imminent. They immersed themselves more than ever in tasting the happiness that only Vishvambhar's presence could bring them. In these final days the *kirtans* were sweeter, the glances more laden with love, the exchanges deeper than ever before.

· · · · · · · ·

THE WINTER'S DAY OF MAKARA-SANKRANTI DAWNED, when the sun entered Capricorn. Vishvambhar whispered to Nityananda: "Tonight I will leave. I will go to Katwa where a pure-hearted monk, Keshava Bharati, is staying. From him I will accept the order of *sannyasa*.[14] Only five people are to be told. They are my mother, Gadadhar, Brahmananda, Chandrashekhar, and my dear Mukunda."

That day, the *kirtans* were blissful and many devotees came to gaze at Vishvambhar, drinking in his beauty. None, except Nityananda and the five, knew he was to leave that very night. They all brought flower garlands to offer their Lord. One by one he called each of them forward so that he could receive their garlands, and in return lovingly placed a garland around each one's neck. Surrounded by a sea of bright faces, Vishvambhar felt boundless love as they were all carried in an ocean of bliss.

"Talk of Krishna, worship Krishna, sing Krishna's name. Think only of Krishna. If you love me, sing only of Lord Krishna and no one else. Whether asleep or awake, or eating your meals, think only of Krishna day and night and with your mouths speak only of him." After saying these last words, Vishvambhar told them all to go home. They left full of joy, unaware of why he spoke to them like this.

Shridhar appeared at the end of his long day in the market, carrying a large squash; beaming with pleasure, he offered it to his master.

"Shridhar, where did you find this?" laughed Vishvambhar, but inwardly he thought, "Tomorrow I will not be here. I must accept this last offering and eat it tonight." Someone else had brought some milk, so he asked his mother to prepare a meal.

"Cook the squash together with the milk—that will be good."

Late in the night, the *kirtan* drew to a close and the few who were still present sat down to eat together. When only two hours of darkness remained,

Vishvambhar sent everyone to bed and he lay down, pretending to sleep. Soon all was quiet. In the darkness he opened his eyes, took a deep breath and sat up, ready to depart. Beside him, Gadadhar stirred. Aware that his master was leaving, he rose to accompany him.

"I go alone, Gadadhar. That is my wish," whispered Vishvambhar.

Silently he moved to the door, but there on the threshold sat his mother, waiting for him with an aching heart. He sank down beside her, embraced her tightly, and spoke softly of his love for her. He reminded her how from birth she had taught him all he knew; how she had filled his life with joy; and how he could never repay her love.

"The Supreme Lord brings us together, and by his will we are separated. Who can understand his ways? I will soon be back."

Sachi listened, unable to speak as tears flowed silently down her cheeks.

Placing his hand on her heart, he repeated, "You are very dear to me. I am with you always." Taking the dust from her feet and placing it on his head, a sign of deep respect, he walked around her with folded hands and quickly disappeared into the night.

·······

SACHI SAT MOTIONLESS. Dawn crept through the air and devotees began to stir. Some of Vishvambhar's friends came looking for him and found Sachi outside his door.

"Mother, why do you sit here?" spoke gentle Shrivas. At first she gave no answer, only tears. Then she found her voice.

"My Lord has left me. Now I belong to Vishnu. Vishnu's possessions belong to his devotees. You, my dear Vaishnavas, can do with me as you like, for my son has gone."

The close associates were stunned. As word spread, they gave themselves over to weeping, laying their heads on one another's shoulders, lying on the floor, sitting in corners with their heads in their hands. Hearing their sobbing, others came to find out what had happened. Soon all of Navadvip knew that Vishvambhar had left to become a *sannyasi*. The whole town was in mourning. Even those who had mocked him cried out in remorse, falling to the ground, "What a chance we have missed! We were sinners and did not understand his greatness."

·······

VISHVAMBHAR WALKED SWIFTLY TO THE GANGES and swam to the opposite shore, then hurried along the road to reach Katwa by late afternoon. There, as arranged, he was met by his five companions, Nityananda, Gadadhar, Mukunda, Chandrashekhar, and Brahmananda. Together they went to Keshava Bharati and told him why they had come. When he understood he was being asked to offer *sannyasa* to the young Vishvambhar, he was hesitant. To invest such a beautiful youth with the ancient order of renunciation would burden a young man of his age with a vow he would find hard to keep.[15]

As crowds materialized to see the famous Vishvambhar, and as they learned of his intention and saw his beauty, they too were sorry that he should be renouncing the world at his tender age. They looked on in awe as the devotees chanted and danced in ecstasy.

"How will his wife and mother continue without him?" said the women as they wept. "How will they even stay alive?"

When the *kirtan* ended, Keshava Bharati said he felt unqualified to initiate such an exalted person. Vishvambhar begged his help to become a servant of Krishna, and at last the venerable *sannyasi* agreed. Soon, night fell and they rested.

The following morning, while a feast was prepared, a large crowd encircled Vishvambhar to watch the ceremony. A barber was brought forward and sat facing him, ready to shave his long, curling locks. Tearfully the barber took up his razor in his trembling hand and raised it to Vishvambhar's head. Amid cries of dismay from the crowd and wailing from the women, he faltered and could not go on. Some of the devotees fainted. Undeterred, Vishvambhar jumped to his feet, asking Mukunda to sing, leading everyone in chanting. Vishvambhar danced with them, swaying and trembling in ecstasy, weeping streams of tears, and lifting the crowd into his mood of love for Krishna.

After some time, while Mukunda continued singing, Vishvambhar sat down again and spoke to the barber, giving him the strength to do his work. One by one, Vishvambhar's dark, curling locks fell to the ground, each to be treasured by some fortunate devotee. His head was anointed with sandalwood oil, and all gasped to see that he glowed more luminously than ever before.

Then the *sannyasa* initiation began. Keshava Bharati was unsure how to initiate so exalted a person. He believed the Divine Lord himself was seated before him. So Vishvambhar leaned forward and whispered into his ear the initiation mantra, prompting him to proceed. By thus giving the mantra to Keshava Bharati, in effect he made him his disciple. All Keshava Bharati had to do was whisper the same mantra in Vishvambhar's ear in return, and the formality was complete. This, he did.

Vishvambhar put on a new saffron cloth and was given a *sannyasa* staff and an alms pot, as was the tradition. He stood before the multitude, with ecstatic tears in his eyes, his beauty shining for everyone to see.

Finally came the choice of name. The normal custom would be for the initiate to adopt the name of his guru, in this case Bharati. But Keshava Bharati was reluctant to name so exalted a person as his disciple. So he searched for a suitable alternative and received divine inspiration.

"You will inspire the whole world to chant Krishna's name, and you will make the world come alive with the sound of chanting. Therefore, I name you Sri Krishna Chaitanya." These words were greeted by everyone with a joyful cry of "Hari!"

The new *sannyasi* liked his name and bowed before his initiator with gratitude. Everyone thought the name was perfect. The barber, still weeping, was congratulated; from that day he abandoned his profession. Amidst joyous confusion, at the end of his twenty-fourth year, Vishvambhar became the glorious and exalted *sannyasi*, Sri Krishna Chaitanya, and embarked on his mission to preach the glories of the holy name of Krishna to people everywhere.

BOOK THREE

Traveling &
Teaching

Leaving Home

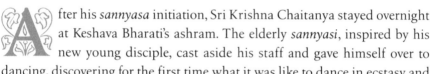fter his *sannyasa* initiation, Sri Krishna Chaitanya stayed overnight at Keshava Bharati's ashram. The elderly *sannyasi*, inspired by his new young disciple, cast aside his staff and gave himself over to dancing, discovering for the first time what it was like to dance in ecstasy and cry out for Krishna. Many souls joined their ecstatic *kirtan* and were blessed with the same good fortune.

In the morning, Krishna Chaitanya said farewell to Keshava Bharati and thanked him for his momentous gift of initiation into the order of *sannyasa*. Then he set off on foot, walking westward accompanied by a large crowd, many of whom were in tears at the prospect of losing him. Now that he had renounced the world, his intention was to travel to Vrindavan. As he followed the path, he danced and ceaselessly sang Krishna's names. From time to time he was overcome with ecstatic emotions and sat weeping beside the road. Whenever he stopped, people crowded around. Hearing his sobs they felt their hearts would break. Eventually Nityananda asked him to bless them and sent them all home. Continuing with only Nityananda, Gadadhar, Chandrashekhar, and Mukunda for company, Krishna Chaitanya entered Radhadesh, the region on the western bank of the Ganges.

For three days Chaitanya wandered in Radhadesh, thinking he was on his way to Vrindavan. In reality, he had no idea where he was. Nityananda wanted to lure him back for one last meeting with the Vaishnavas at Advaita's house in

Shantipur. He managed to direct Chaitanya in a circle, so that eventually they returned to the bank of the Ganges.

"Here is the River Yamuna that flows through Vrindavan," said Nityananda. "You have only to follow the course of the river and you will soon reach Krishna's home."

Chaitanya heard these words with joy, believing them to be true. He embraced Chandrashekhar and gave him a message to carry back to Navadvip.

"Tell the Vaishnavas I am on my way to Vrindavan. Please do not be unhappy, for I will love you all birth after birth." Then he began to follow the river.

Nityananda spoke with Chandrashekhar privately, asking him to tell Sachi and the devotees to go to Advaita's house in Shantipur and prepare to receive Chaitanya there. Chandrashekhar hurried back to Navadvip with his messages. When he arrived, he found everyone gathered around Sachi, weeping and chanting Krishna's names. He explained Nityananda's plan, and encouraged them all to go to Shantipur, where for the last time they could see their beloved Vishvambhar before he left to embark on his new life.

········

While Chaitanya continued on his way, Nityananda went ahead to Advaita's house. He persuaded Advaita to take a boat upriver and meet Chaitanya, who was walking along the bank. So, to Chaitanya's surprise, he encountered Advaita coming his way in a boat.

"Advaita, you too are in Vrindavan!"

"Wherever you are, Lord, there is Vrindavan," replied Advaita, smiling, "even here on the banks of the Ganges. Now let me take you to my home, where many friends await you." Realizing he had been tricked, Chaitanya laughed and accepted Advaita's invitation to board the boat.

At Advaita's house, a wonderful meal had been prepared. Sri Krishna Chaitanya was now a *sannyasi* and he wanted to live as *sannyasis* did: renouncing worldly comforts to be fully dedicated to the service of God. But Advaita had always wanted to receive Chaitanya as a guest in his house, and to feed him sumptuously in a way that befitted the Lord of the Universe. In obedience to his friend's wishes, Chaitanya sat down beside Nityananda and ate the opulent meal he was offered. Then he allowed himself to be led to a comfortable bed where Advaita massaged his feet. Chaitanya accepted all this in good humor, while Advaita and his godbrother Nityananda joked with him, as all three of them enjoyed the irony of the situation.

The people of Navadvip had, in a sense, lost their glorious Vishvambhar, but now that Chandrashekhar brought news of Vishvambhar's initiation, they all wanted to see him in his new garb as a renounced monk. Sachi, having fasted and wept for days, also wanted to meet her son in his new role. Even Vishvambhar's former critics, who had driven him to become a *sannyasi*, wanted to see him. Consequently, a great tide of souls set off from Navadvip in the direction of Shantipur. Thousands gathered around Advaita's house, waiting for a glimpse of Chaitanya, and loudly chanted Krishna's names.

Krishna Chaitanya heard the crowd singing and went outside to see them. Beholding the beautiful young *sannyasi*, the people bowed down in the dust with utmost love and reverence.

"Save us! Save us!" they cried aloud.

Observing the vast gathering stretching as far as the eye could see, Chaitanya was amazed. Among them were his close friends, who stepped forward to embrace him. Advaita started to sing, joined by Nityananda and Haridas, and a tumultuous *kirtan* continued late into the night. Chaitanya sang with them, and as he sang, his ecstatic love for Krishna increased more and more, until he fell to the ground and was unable to continue dancing. Then, Mukunda, sitting next to Chaitanya, sang sweet verses to him about the love between Radha and Krishna. Their effect was to send Chaitanya into deeper ecstasy; he lost all control of his body and mind, so much so that the devotees were anxious and Advaita suspended the festival for the night, taking Chaitanya indoors to lie down and rest.

The following day Sachi arrived from Navadvip. Her son fell at her feet in love and respect. Seeing his shaven head without its long, curling locks, with tear-filled eyes she kissed him and showered him with motherly love. Advaita welcomed Sachi into his house, and she took charge of the cooking for her son and his companions. Chaitanya stayed there for ten days, during which time there was much to discuss about his future.

"Don't be cruel to me, as your elder brother was," Sachi begged. "He left home forever, without sending me news of his travels. If the same happens with you I will surely die."

"Mother dear, my body belongs to you. Whatever you ask, I will obey," he promised.

It was decided with Sachi's approval that Chaitanya should not go to Vrindavan, which was far away. Instead he would go to Jagannath Puri, the holy city in the state of Orissa. Puri was home to the magnificent temple of

Jagannath, the deity of Krishna who displayed his majesty as Lord of the Universe. The ancient temple stood on the edge of the Bay of Bengal, three hundred miles south of Navadvip. News could regularly pass between there and Navadvip; devotees could easily visit Chaitanya there; and he might also visit them in return.

While they were all together for those last few days in Bengal, devotees got the chance to spend personal time with Chaitanya in the day, and at night they joined him in chanting and dancing. In those *kirtans* he expressed his love without restraint, one moment leaping in the air, the next rolling on the ground, then weeping and embracing his friends. On the final day, he sat on Vishnu's altar in the midst of everyone and showed for the last time his glory as Lord of Lords.

"I am Krishna, I am Balaram, and I am Rama," he declared. "I am Vishnu, Brahma, and Shiva. Countless universes emanate from me. I kill the demons and protect my devotees. You, my dear devotees, are one with me. You are my father, mother, friend, son, and brother. You are with me birth after birth and we are never separated, not even for a moment."

One last time he went with them to bathe in the Ganges. Then they all sat together for a final meal. In the center sat Chaitanya and Nityananda; seeing them, people were reminded of Krishna and Balaram sharing lunch in the forest with their cowherd friends.

Early the next morning, Chaitanya said farewell to his mother, bowing humbly before her, and then set off for Jagannath Puri. He took with him Nityananda, Mukunda, and two other companions. Many followed him and would not let him out of their sight. After a short time he turned to them.

"I must go now, but in a little while I will come back to visit you. Please do not be unhappy. Go to your homes and always chant Krishna's names. I will never leave you." Then he spoke to Advaita. "I depend upon you, my dear Advaita, to guide the devotees. Please see that my mother is taken care of."

With these words Sri Krishna Chaitanya embraced Advaita and quickly left, heading south with his four companions. With tears in their eyes, the devotees comforted one another and returned to their homes.

Journey to Puri

Chaitanya was at last free to embark on life as a *sannyasi*. His path lay south, in the direction of Jagannath Puri. On the way, he and his companions would have to pass through territory patrolled by hostile Muslim forces. The party carried no money because they wished to depend entirely on Krishna for their food and shelter, and because money would be an invitation to thieves. Each night they sheltered in someone's home.

As he traveled, Chaitanya hardly knew whether it was day or night, or which way the path lay. He was absorbed in thoughts of Krishna, and in the prospect of seeing Krishna's form of Jagannath. Following the Ganges, they came to the town of Chatrabhoga. Here the river divided into many streams before flowing into the Bay of Bengal. The governor of the district, Ramachandra Khan, came out to greet Chaitanya. He invited the travelers to his home and offered to guide them safely through the dangerous territory that lay ahead.

In the dead of night they were led to the riverbank, where a boat had been made ready. Climbing aboard they slid out into the smooth-flowing waters of Mother Ganges. In the darkness, Mukunda sang Krishna's names as shadows drifted by along the banks. The boatman feared crocodiles and pirates, and begged Mukunda to sing quietly lest they attract attention.

"Have no fear! We are protected by the sound of Krishna's names," assured Chaitanya.

As dawn broke, they reached the borders of Orissa, and the boatman steered ashore at Sri Prayag Ghat, where Chaitanya first set foot on Orissan soil. They bathed in the Ganges and paid their respects to Lord Shiva at his temple there. A *sannyasi* was expected to beg for alms, so Chaitanya went on his own from house to house asking for rice and vegetables. Whoever saw him was captivated by his sincerity and effulgence, and in no time he returned with his arms full. When they saw how much he had brought, his companions smiled, realizing that they would not go hungry on their journey. After cooking and eating, they listened to Mukunda singing late into the night.

Resuming their travels early the next morning, they came to a tollgate, where the collector demanded payment to let them pass. Chaitanya thought he would be prevented from reaching Jagannath and began to cry. Moved by his tears, the collector let him pass, but insisted the others should pay. When he saw his companions barred, he sat down alone by the road and wept even more. His cries were enough to melt anyone's heart. Bowing before the young *sannyasi* and himself crying, the collector let them through.

They traveled onward through Orissa for several days, until they reached the River Bharginadi, close to Jagannath Puri. Chaitanya had with him a bamboo staff, the symbol of his *sannyasa* order. He had entrusted this staff to Nityananda to look after. Nityananda disliked the staff, since he had never agreed with Chaitanya's becoming a *sannyasi* in the first place, and to his mind the burden of such an outward symbol was entirely unnecessary for an exalted soul like Chaitanya. Deciding to get rid of it, he broke the staff into three pieces and threw it into the river.[16] When Chaitanya found that his staff was missing, he asked Nityananda where it was and learned it had been broken and thrown away.

"This staff was my only companion and now you have destroyed it," he protested in anger. "From here, I will travel alone."

Chaitanya strode ahead on his own, walking quickly and purposefully. In the distance he soon saw the pinnacle of the Jagannath temple, its monumental stonework towering above the waving palms, with its red flag flying in the sea breeze. He walked with mounting excitement, anticipating the sight of Jagannath, the awesome sacred form of Krishna who lived inside the great temple, served by hundreds of priests and worshipped by countless pilgrims. Behind him trailed his companions, anxious not to lose sight of their beloved master.

Meeting Sarvabhauma

Chaitanya arrived alone at the Lion Gate of the great temple of Puri and went inside. As the temple guards watched with fascination, he passed across the outer courtyard, through the next gateway, and into the inner precinct of the temple. To the guards, he appeared like an effulgent figure, who seemed to float, as if unaware of his surroundings.

They saw him enter the engulfing shadows of the inner temple and stop in front of the main altar. There, illuminated by the glow of flickering oil lamps, and attended by priests who moved silently in the background, stood three immense sacred images about eight feet tall, the focus of devotion in the great temple. These divine forms were Krishna, called Jagannath (Lord of the Universe), with his sister, Subhadra, and his mighty brother, Balaram. The *sannyasi's* eyes drank in Jagannath's huge face, his great, circular eyes and broad red smile, and saw in his extended hands the disc and conch, symbols of Vishnu's power and mercy.

For a moment the golden *sannyasi* stood mesmerized, his body trembling with ecstasy and tears flowing down his cheeks. His breath came in gasps as he tried to call out the name of Jagannath. Then, with a cry, he fell to the floor like a stone, unconscious.

The guards rushed forward and would have handled him roughly, but were stopped by a diminutive and dignified elder man who emerged from the shadows. Stooping, he studied the golden figure sprawled before him. He could see at once by his noble features and luminous aura that he was no ordinary *sannyasi*. He sat beside him on the stone floor, shielding him from the guards and waiting for him to regain consciousness. As he waited, he noticed with alarm that the *sannyasi* did not appear to be breathing. The elder called for help and had the young man carried to a side room. There, he knelt beside the unconscious body and held a piece of cotton to his nostrils. To his relief, he saw that the cotton fibers moved slightly, indicating that he was still alive. He continued to study the beautiful monk, whose soft features and body were suspended in perfect stillness. He concluded that he must be in the deepest ecstasy, called *suddipta*, in which the classic symptoms of spiritual rapture were all present to the highest degree. With great care, he raised the unconscious Chaitanya and, helped by temple attendants, carried him to his house.

Chaitanya's rescuer was Sarvabhauma Bhattacharya, an elder citizen of the town and the most respected teacher in Puri. He was celebrated as one of the greatest authorities of his day in the philosophy of Advaita Vedanta, the sublime teaching of the great unity of all life in Brahman, pure spirit; people came from all over India to learn from him.

Nityananda and Chaitanya's other companions arrived at the main gate of the temple, where they inquired if anyone had seen a tall and handsome young *sannyasi*. By good fortune, an old friend of Mukunda's happened to be there, a person named Gopinath, who had visited Navadvip and was himself Chaitanya's devotee. He told them about the appearance of an unknown *sannyasi* who had fainted as he came before Jagannath.

After explaining all this, Gopinath led Chaitanya's companions to Sarvabhauma's house. With relief, they found their master there, lying unconscious but cared for.

Sarvabhauma welcomed the devotees and introduced himself. Once they were assured that Chaitanya was in safe hands, they too went to the temple to see Jagannath. Since he was worshipped as protector of the town of Jagannath Puri, they wanted to offer prayers to him. They stood before Jagannath and were blessed with flower garlands given to them by the priests. After briefly seeing the Lord of Puri, the devotees were able to return to Chaitanya. They found him lying peacefully where they had left him, still breathing only slightly. They gathered around him and chanted Krishna's names. Soon he opened his eyes, got up, and looked around him.

"Welcome to my home, O master," said Sarvabhauma respectfully. "Today you are my guest. Please have your bath, and then I will give you some sacred food from Jagannath's temple."

Sarvabhauma's house was a short walk from the ocean. Gopinath led Chaitanya and his devotees to the long, sandy beach, which was the customary bathing place for the people of Puri. They swam in the sea and returned refreshed to Sarvabhauma's house for lunch. After the meal, Sarvabhauma came forward to introduce himself to his guests.

"Namo Narayanaya," intoned the teacher, using the traditional words to greet a *sannyasi*. These words addressed Chaitanya as the Supreme Narayana, name of Vishnu, implying he had realized his oneness with God.

"Krishna *matir astu*," replied Chaitanya, meaning, "Let your mind be upon Krishna." By this exchange they each identified themselves, Sarvabhauma as a philosopher of Advaita, oneness, who considered all beings as one with God, and Chaitanya as a devotee of Krishna who looked upon all as loving servants of God.

Sarvabhauma was himself originally from Navadvip, and soon discovered that Chaitanya's grandfather had been a friend of his own father. Learning this filled him with fatherly affection for the young monk. He made arrangements for him to stay in his house as long as he liked, and delegated his brother-in-law, Gopinath, to look after all Chaitanya's needs. Furthermore, he decided it was his duty to teach his adopted nephew, giving him the benefit of his personal instruction in Advaita Vedanta, so that he could be well established in his renunciation, safe from the temptations that might beset a handsome and charismatic young monk.

When Sarvabhauma told Gopinath of his offer to teach Chaitanya, Gopinath was indignant.

"Sri Krishna Chaitanya is no ordinary person: he is the Supreme Lord himself. Why should he need instruction from you?"

"My dear Gopinath, I readily accept Sri Krishna Chaitanya as a wonderful devotee of Krishna. But where is the evidence that he is an incarnation of God as described in the scriptures?"

Gopinath hotly debated whether or not Chaitanya was in fact an incarnation of God. His arguments did not convince the teacher, who insisted on inviting Chaitanya to be his student, suggesting that they meet at the great Jagannath temple. When Chaitanya heard of Sarvabhauma's invitation, he waived aside Gopinath's objections.

"Sarvabhauma Bhattacharya is very kind to me. He just wants to help me to be a good *sannyasi*. Where is the harm?"

One day, not long afterward, Sarvabhauma led his student to a quiet corner in the precincts of the temple. There, to respect Chaitanya's status as a *sannyasi*, he arranged a comfortable seat for him, while uncharacteristically the teacher sat on the floor at his feet.

"Now we shall begin our lessons. For your own good, listen as I recite the *Vedanta Sutra* with the commentary of the great Shankara. Learn from what I say." With this he began lecturing. His classes lasted for seven days, during which time Chaitanya listened attentively. When the teacher reached the end of his lectures, he was perplexed.

"For seven days you have listened in silence. Why have you not spoken? Have you understood anything I've said?"

"I am a fool," replied Chaitanya, "and I am not interested in Vedanta philosophy. But because you tell me it is my duty as a *sannyasi*, I am trying my best to hear what you say."

"If you don't follow what I'm saying, then why don't you ask me to explain?"

"I understand the *sutras* themselves—their meaning is clear. But Shankara's commentary obscures them like a cloud. It seems to me that his commentary avoids the essential meaning of the *sutras* by interpreting them indirectly."

Chaitanya then explained the *sutras* in a simple and straightforward way that didn't touch on Sarvabhauma's elaborate explanations. He concluded by saying that Shankara's commentary, far from clarifying the truth, misled the followers of the *Vedas* into thinking of God as impersonal, and in doing so damaged their faith.

At first, Sarvabhauma resisted Chaitanya's arguments with arguments of his own, but eventually he fell silent. For some time, he listened in rapt attention, stunned by the truth and harmony of the young *sannyasi*'s words. Finally,

Chaitanya mentioned a well-known verse from the *Srimad Bhagavatam* that described the most enlightened souls, those who have forsaken all attraction to the material world.

> Even those who are self-satisfied *(atma-rama)*, who are no longer moved by material desires, offer loving service to Krishna whose wonderful qualities and activities attract all souls.

This verse implied that love for Krishna was beyond the material plane; the soul who had given up all attraction to the world of illusion was still attracted to Krishna, because Krishna lay beyond the illusion. Chaitanya invited the learned teacher to explain the verse, so Sarvabhauma analyzed the Sanskrit in nine different ways. When Sarvabhauma had finished, Chaitanya supplied sixty-four further explanations of the verse, without touching on his teacher's interpretations. Hearing these, the teacher was dumbfounded. His heart changed. Believing he was in the presence of the Supreme Lord himself, he renounced his pride and called for mercy.

Chaitanya granted Sarvabhauma a vision of his Vishnu form, and then revealed his form as Krishna playing a flute. When he saw these wonderful things, Sarvabhauma fell full length on the floor in love and adoration, holding on to Chaitanya's feet and weeping as he spoke.

"Today I have found the thief who stole my heart."

"Rise, Sarvabhauma," said Chaitanya, placing his hand on Sarvabhauma's head. "I have shown you this form because you are very dear to me. I came here to Puri just to deliver you. Though in this life you have been a scholar of Advaita Vedanta, in many previous lives you were my devoted servant."

With folded hands, weeping and trembling with joy, Sarvabhauma composed spontaneous Sanskrit verses in praise of his new master. Before they parted, Chaitanya asked Sarvabhauma to keep his vision a secret.

The next day, Sarvabhauma came with a question. His pride had evaporated and he fell at Chaitanya's feet as his student.

"In offering devotional service to the Lord, what is the most important practice?"

Chaitanya gave him the same instruction he had given Shuklambar in Navadvip, and often repeated since: "Chanting Krishna's names is the only means of success in this age. No other means—either study, or penance, or good works—is necessary to achieve salvation."

After becoming the teacher of Sarvabhauma, who was known all over India as Prabhu, a renowned master of Vedanta, Chaitanya began to be known as Mahaprabhu, the Great Master. His devotees were overjoyed at Sarvabhauma's transformation. Mukunda overheard Sarvabhauma singing Sanskrit verses he had composed in Chaitanya's honor, and wrote two of them on the outer wall of his room for all to see. These two verses were learned by Chaitanya's devotees.

> I surrender myself to the Supreme Lord who has appeared in this world as the ocean of mercy, Sri Krishna Chaitanya, to teach knowledge, detachment, and devotional service to himself.
>
> The ancient science of devotional service was lost over the course of time and Sri Krishna Chaitanya has come to revive it. May my consciousness, like a honeybee, find rest at his lotus feet.

The people of Jagannath Puri heard how the young *sannyasi* from Bengal had profoundly influenced their most respected citizen; they observed Chaitanya Mahaprabhu as he walked about their town, blissfully chanting Krishna's names and showing love to all he met. When they saw his spiritual beauty and felt his love, their hearts were captivated. They called him the moving Jagannath: one Jagannath stood in their great temple to receive their worship—now they had a second Jagannath who walked among them.

Travels in the South

One evening, by the light of the full moon, Mahaprabhu went down to the seashore. In Jagannatha Puri a group of close companions were collecting around him, and they went with him. Cooled by the breeze, they sat together on the beach and talked of Krishna. The rays of the moon sparkled on the ocean waves, reminding Mahaprabhu of the Yamuna River flowing through the forest of Vrindavan. They stayed all night on the beach, singing to Krishna and dancing. When Mahaprabhu danced, powerful emotions swept through his body; he shed tears, laughed, embraced his friends, and sometimes rolled in the sand. All of them cherished the memory of Mahaprabhu and his *kirtan* by the ocean.

After he had been in Puri for little more than a month, Mahaprabhu called his devotees together and took their hands.

"You are all dear friends to me. You brought me here to the temple of Jagannath, and I never want to lose your company. But now I ask a favor of you. Let me go on pilgrimage through South India; while I am there, I will also look for my brother Vishvarup. I want to go alone, but I will soon return."

Speaking for them all, Nityananda protested.

"If you must go, then at least take some of us with you."

Mahaprabhu was persuaded to take with him a single companion, a simple man named Krishnadas who would look after his personal needs. So it was decided, but Sarvabhauma was unhappy.

"After many lifetimes I have found you, and now you are leaving me," the teacher lamented. In response to his pleas, Mahaprabhu delayed for a few days, staying with Sarvabhauma at his house. When it was finally time for him to go, Sarvabhauma made a special request.

"In the town of Vidyanagara on the River Godavari you will meet a man named Ramananda Raya, who is governor of Madras. Although he is apparently preoccupied with material affairs, he is a highly advanced devotee of Krishna with deep understanding of devotional service. Please meet him— I am sure you will appreciate his company." Mahaprabhu promised he would find him.

As he watched his master leave, Sarvabhauma fainted and had to be helped back to his house. Others followed Mahaprabhu as far as he would allow them, though they too were left behind, weeping as they watched him leave. Despite missing his friends, he was determined to travel alone. He walked purposefully toward the South with only Krishnadas following behind him.

········

AS HE WALKED ON HIS WAY, Mahaprabhu sang with ecstasy. One favorite chant was always on his lips:

Krishna Krishna Krishna Krishna Krishna Krishna Krishna he
Krishna Krishna Krishna Krishna Krishna Krishna Krishna he
Krishna Krishna Krishna Krishna Krishna Krishna raksha mam
Krishna Krishna Krishna Krishna Krishna Krishna pahi mam
Rama Raghava Rama Raghava Rama Raghava raksha mam
Krishna Keshava Krishna Keshava Krishna Keshava pahi mam

In awe, the devotees worshipped him. They bathed him with pots of Ganges water, offered him fruits and flowers and the arati *ceremony. Running here and there, they gathered food to prepare wonderful dishes for their Lord (see page 58).*

Although Nityananda was injured by the brothers Jagai and Madhai, he was unafraid and stood his ground, determined to redeem them. Vishvambhar quickly came to his defence (see page 63).

Vishvambhar renounced household life to become a sannyasi. *He told his tearful mother he would always be with her, then he disappeared into the night (see page 75).*

His head shaven and wearing new saffron cloth, he received a sannyasa *staff and an alms pot. Standing before the multitude with ecstatic tears in his eyes, he became the glorious and exalted* sannyasi *Sri Krishna Chaitanya (see page 77).*

Krishna Chaitanya set off on foot accompanied by a large crowd. As he followed the path, he danced and ceaselessly sang Krishna's names, overcome with ecstatic emotions (see page 81).

Sachi arrived from Navadvip. Seeing her son's shaven head without its long, curling locks, with tear-filled eyes she kissed him and showered him with motherly love (see page 83).

Chaitanya saw in the distance the pinnacle of the Jagannath temple, its monumental stonework towering above the waving palms, its red flag flying in the sea breeze (see page 86).

With a cry, he fell unconscious to the floor. The temple guards rushed forward and would have handled him roughly but were stopped by a dignified elder man who emerged from the shadows (see page 87).

With relief, they found their master lying unconscious but breathing slightly. They gathered
around him and chanted Krishna's names. Soon he opened his eyes, got up and looked
around him (see page 87).

Sarvabhauma led his student to a quiet corner in the precincts of the temple, where he
lectured to him on the Vedanta Sutra. Chaitanya listened in silence for seven days, then
taught the sutras back to Sarvabhauma (see page 89).

Chaitanya granted Sarvabhauma a vision of his Vishnu form, and then revealed his form as Krishna playing a flute. When he saw these wonderful things Sarvabhauma fell on the floor in love and adoration (see page 90).

One evening, by the light of the full moon, Mahaprabhu went down to the seashore with his companions.
They stayed all night on the beach, singing to Krishna and dancing (see page 91).

Ramananda Raya saw the saffron-robed sannyasi, his golden skin glowing and his eyes wide like lotus petals. Deep feelings of love awakened in their hearts as they embraced and wept (see page 95).

Mahaprabhu was joined in Puri by three close companions: Svarup Damodar, who sang to him devotional poems; his lifelong friend Gadadhar, who read to him the stories of Krishna; and Govinda, who became his personal servant (see page 98).

This could be translated as: "Krishna, protect me and maintain me. Rama, descendant of Raghu, protect me. Krishna, killer of the Keshi demon, maintain me."

While he traveled in the South, Mahaprabhu manifested powers he had previously kept hidden. As he passed through each village, people followed him and joined in singing Krishna's names. He would embrace them, transforming their hearts and overwhelming them with love for God. These people returned to their villages and continued singing; whoever heard them sing also became a devotee of Krishna. Through Mahaprabhu's potency, Krishna consciousness spread wherever he went.

One such village was Kurmakshetra, where an ancient temple was dedicated to the avatar of Vishnu named Kurma. Here a *brahmana* invited Mahaprabhu into his home and washed his feet, then cooked for him. After the meal, the *brahmana* shared Mahaprabhu's leftovers with his family.

"Lord, you have blessed me and my family today," said the *brahmana*. "Please let me leave my home and family and come with you. I can no longer tolerate the waves of misery caused by material life."

When he heard these words, Mahaprabhu corrected the *brahmana*.

"Never say such things. Stay at home and chant Krishna's names. Tell whomever you meet about Krishna's teachings. I ask you to become a guru and free your people."

Wherever he received hospitality during his travels, Mahaprabhu stayed long enough to give the householders these same essential teachings.

He reached the banks of the Godavari River, near Vidyanagara. There he bathed in her sacred waters and rested beneath a tree. While he was sitting beside the river, remembering the Yamuna in Vrindavan and quietly chanting Krishna's names, he saw a large group approaching. A man of importance was being carried in a palanquin, attended by musicians, priests, and servants. He had come to the river to bathe and to perform a Vedic rite. Mahaprabhu understood this was Ramananda Raya, governor of Madras—the very person recommended to him by Sarvabhauma.

Mahaprabhu remained sitting where he was, waiting to speak with him. The governor saw the saffron-robed *sannyasi* sitting quietly on his own, his golden skin glowing and his eyes wide like lotus petals. Spontaneously, the governor came over to show respect. As he came near he found himself dazzled as if by the light of many suns. He dropped to the ground before the effulgent *sannyasi* and stretched full length in the sand in humility.

They both rose to their feet and Mahaprabhu asked if this was Ramananda Raya. The governor introduced himself, saying he was an unworthy servant, and Mahaprabhu responded with a warm embrace. Though in this life they had never met, deep feelings of love awakened in their hearts as they embraced and wept.

Some of Ramananda's entourage were touched by the sight of their leader with this young *sannyasi*, and began to chant Krishna's names. The *brahmanas* attending Ramananda, however, disapproved of a *sannyasi* embracing a governor, and of a highly placed man like Ramananda losing all composure and weeping like a baby. Seeing their critical gaze, Mahaprabhu and Ramananda restrained their feelings and moved some distance away to sit down and talk. They talked first of Sarvabhauma, whose kindness Ramananda praised for recommending that Mahaprabhu find him. Then they arranged to meet in private as soon as possible. A *brahmana* who lived nearby invited Mahaprabhu to stay in his house, so it was decided that they would meet there.

That evening, Ramananda came to the *brahmana*'s house and withdrew with Mahaprabhu to a quiet place where they entered a deep conversation. Mahaprabhu had heard from Sarvabhauma of the depth of Ramananda's wisdom, and he saw for himself the man's qualities. Adopting the role of a student, he placed a series of questions to Ramananda. He began by asking him to recite verses from scripture about the ultimate goal of life.

Ramananda, being a governor, replied with a verse from the *Vishnu Purana* that prescribed the general good for society: that people should carry out their social duties and in time they would be rewarded with increased understanding of God.

This was not what Mahaprabhu wanted to hear—he wanted to go deeper. He urged Ramananda to say something else. Ramananda quoted the *Bhagavad Gita*: "Whatever you do, eat, offer or give away, and whatever hardship you undergo, offer it to me." By this he suggested that not only should people do their duty, but they should do it for the sake of Krishna.

Again Mahaprabhu asked him to go further. Ramananda cited another verse from the *Gita*, in which Krishna recommends giving up duties, saying: "Abandon all kinds of religion and surrender to me alone. I will free you from all sinful reactions. Do not fear." Still, this did not satisfy Mahaprabhu; he wanted to hear about positive spiritual engagement rather than renunciation. Ramananda went further, citing a verse from the *Srimad Bhagavatam*: "The

Lord is conquered by those who, regardless of their position in life, simply hear about him from his devotees."

"Yes, this is right," replied Mahaprabhu.

All his life he had taught that people should try to reach God through devotion alone. They did not need to practice pious work, pursuit of knowledge, or renunciation of this world; they could simply hear about Krishna from devotees and so learn to love him. Once Ramananda had reached this general principle, Mahaprabhu urged him to go deeper and describe devotion to Krishna. Together they discussed how love for God is the highest goal of life; how a soul's loving relationship with God develops from passive adoration through successive stages of intimacy; and how eventually it can manifest as unconditional love between lover and beloved.

Ramananda Raya was expert in understanding advanced love for God, but no one had ever asked him such penetrating questions as Mahaprabhu now asked. He felt as if his tongue was vibrating like a stringed instrument played by the Lord of all. Night after night they talked of the love between Krishna and his devotees, as if they were mining rare gems from the depths of the earth. They spoke of how Krishna responds to his devotee's wishes; if, for example, his devotee wants to look after him, Krishna plays the role of a child, as he had for Yashoda, who served as his mother in Vrindavan. He would even play the role of lover for those who wished to love him in that most intimate way. Ramananda described the way to this most elevated perfection, which follows in the footsteps of the cowherd girls who dance with Krishna in the eternal forest of Vrindavan.

In their sacred conversation, they reached the ultimate example of Krishna's love: his union with Radha. She was the embodiment of Krishna's purest compassion and ecstasy. When Ramananda began to describe Radha, their talks entered deep into the realms of spiritual mystery. In the darkness of the night, while all around them slept, Mahaprabhu and Ramananda tasted ecstasies unknown in this world as they invoked Radha's presence. As Ramananda spoke, inspired to go ever deeper, he reached places accessible only to the most fortunate souls. At last they could go no further and the door was opened to Mahaprabhu's greatest secret.

Before Ramananda's eyes, Mahaprabhu transformed into Krishna, playing upon his flute. Ramananda saw that Krishna, instead of appearing dark blue, was suffused with the golden luster of Radha. So Ramananda understood the mystery of Mahaprabhu's inner nature: he was both Radha and Krishna combined in one person. When Ramananda saw this he fell into a trance. Mahaprabhu gently awakened him and told him no one else had ever seen this form. He asked that it remain a secret between them only, and then he embraced him.

Mahaprabhu stayed with Ramananda by the River Godavari for ten days. Each night they talked, but still they felt they had hardly begun. When it was time for Ramananda to leave, Mahaprabhu invited him to move permanently to Jagannath Puri, where they could spend their time talking about Krishna. From that day, Ramananda began to plan his withdrawal from government service so that he could devote the remainder of his days to being with Mahaprabhu.

········

IN HIS CONTINUING TRAVELS, Mahaprabhu visited many important holy sites in South India, and wherever he went he taught people about Krishna, changing the course of their lives.

For the four months of the rainy season he stayed in the temple city of Rangakshetra, home to the largest Vishnu temple in India. There he was a guest in the house of Vyenkata Bhatta, who became his disciple. Vyenkata was one of the chief temple priests leading the worship of Vishnu, God as the Supreme Maintainer, in a style of grand opulence. Influenced by Mahaprabhu, he and his family developed a lasting personal devotion to Krishna, who plays his flute and herds cows in the eternal forest of Vrindavan. Many souls heard from Mahaprabhu during his stay with Vyenkata and learned from him to chant Krishna's names.

In this city lived a *brahmana* who used to visit the temple every day to chant the verses of the *Bhagavad Gita*, which contains Krishna's words of love and wisdom to his friend Arjuna. The *brahmana* was a simple man who could neither understand nor properly pronounce the Sanskrit verses. Although educated *brahmanas* made fun of his efforts, he was not deterred from his daily devotion. One day, Mahaprabhu came upon the *brahmana* chanting the *Gita*, and saw that he was weeping and trembling with ecstasy.

"Which part of the *Gita* gives you so much happiness?" asked Mahaprabhu.

"I am illiterate, master, so I do not understand Krishna's words," replied the *brahmana*, "but I chant them because my guru told me to. As I chant I see before me the image of Krishna, who is so kind to his friend Arjuna that he has taken the reins of his chariot and is teaching him. This image fills my eyes with tears and I can think of nothing else."

"You truly understand the *Bhagavad Gita*," said Mahaprabhu, embracing him. Upon receiving this embrace, the *brahmana* cried in astonishment, because he saw before him the very same Krishna whom he daily worshipped. After this, he wanted to be with Mahaprabhu all the time. He visited him daily at Vyenkata's house, and was personally taught many things. Before Mahaprabhu left Rangakshetra, he made the *brahmana* promise not to tell anyone the secret of his divine identity.

········

For two years, Mahaprabhu traveled the length of South India, teaching people about Krishna and asking those whom he taught to also teach others.

"Whether you are a *brahmana*, a *sannyasi,* or a householder," he said, "if you understand the truth about Krishna you can be a guru and teach others." Wherever he went he attracted people to become devotees of Krishna and established the chanting of Krishna's holy names.

On his way back to Jagannath Puri, Mahaprabhu once again stopped at Vidyanagara and spent several more days with Ramananda, continuing their mystical discussions. From there, he returned on the same road by which he had left two years before.

When he reached the edge of Puri, he sent his servant ahead to tell Nityananda of his arrival. Friends hurried out to meet him, crying tears of joy. Together they went first to the temple of Jagannath, where Sarvabhauma fell at Mahaprabhu's feet. Mahaprabhu told him that although he had traveled all over South India he had not found such a wonderful Vaishnava as Sarvabhauma. Then he went to see Jagannath and danced in ecstasy surrounded by his friends, while the priests came out with garlands and sanctified food.

Mahaprabhu was brought to Sarvabhauma's house, where he bathed and ate. While Mahaprabhu had been away, the King of Orissa, Maharaj Prataparudra, had arranged a set of rooms specifically for his use in a house owned by Kashi Mishra. Mahaprabhu's friends led him to these new rooms, where Kashi Mishra received him with great reverence. Everyone stayed up through the night hearing Mahaprabhu's tales of his wonderful experiences in South India.

Visitors from Bengal

For two long years, the devotees in Bengal had been without Vishvambhar, hearing only occasional news of him and waiting to see him again. In his absence, they had carried on with their *kirtans*, gathering in their homes or meeting at the houses of Shrivas and Advaita; sometimes they met in public to chant in the streets as he had taught them to do. Now news reached them that he had returned to Puri; without delay they made preparations to go and see him.

Around this time, Mahaprabhu was joined by three people who became his close companions. One was Svarup Damodar, whom he chose to be his personal assistant. Svarup had originally known Mahaprabhu in Navadvip, and had since moved to Varanasi where he became a *sannyasi*. Now he came to join Mahaprabhu in Puri, and the two were reunited with great affection. Svarup Damodar knew the scriptures well, and he had deep understanding of the spiritual emotions Mahaprabhu was experiencing. He knew how to respond to them, in ways that nobody else could understand, by singing from the devotional poems of Vidyapati, Chandidas, and Jayadev. A second person to join Mahaprabhu was Govinda, who had been servant to Mahaprabhu's guru, Ishvara Puri. Before Ishvara Puri left this world, he had ordered Govinda to devote himself to Mahaprabhu's personal service. The third significant companion was Mahaprabhu's lifelong friend Gadadhar. They had grown up together in Navadvip where they had been inseparable. Now in Puri, Gadadhar used to read to Mahaprabhu from the *Srimad Bhagavatam*, consoling him with stories of Krishna and Krishna's devotees.

Many others joined their master in Puri, too many to mention by name. Each possessed unique qualities and served him in special ways. They came from all over the country, as rivers flow to the sea, and he gave each of them his abiding love and spiritual shelter.

········

THE KING OF ORISSA, MAHARAJ PRATAPARUDRA, was a powerful ruler who was fighting to defend the Hindu kingdom of Orissa from Hussein Shah, the Muslim ruler of neighboring Bengal to the north. The King was a religious man devoted to the service of Jagannath. He returned from a military campaign and heard about a great spiritual personality recently arrived from

Bengal. Even a king was expected to pay his respects to a *sannyasi*, so King Prataparudra asked Sarvabhauma to arrange a meeting with Mahaprabhu. Sarvabhauma told him, however, that it would be difficult to see the *sannyasi* because his vows of renunciation made him reluctant to keep company with a king, a man always in the midst of worldly affairs. Nevertheless, Sarvabhauma promised he would try to help. He repeatedly asked Mahaprabhu to receive the King, but Mahaprabhu was unwilling.

"Even though the King may be a great devotee of Jagannath, it would still be dangerous for me to associate with him," Mahaprabhu said. When Sarvabhauma pressed him, he added, "If you persist with such a suggestion, I will leave this place."

Sarvabhauma was afraid to say anything more and let the subject rest.

The King, who by now had learned all about the glories of Mahaprabhu, was anxious to meet him. He heard that his request had been refused and was despondent.

"Why is it that Sri Chaitanya Mahaprabhu has appeared in this world to free even the most fallen souls like Jagai and Madhai, yet he will not see me? It seems I am the only one not to receive his mercy. Without him, my kingdom seems empty and useless."

Sarvabhauma assured the King that since his devotion for Mahaprabhu was deep, it would surely be rewarded. He must be patient while Sarvabhauma found a way to arrange a meeting.

The King's hopes of meeting Mahaprabhu were raised when Ramananda Raya, with a great retinue of horses, elephants, and soldiers, arrived in Puri to retire. Ramananda went straight to see Mahaprabhu. They embraced, shedding tears of love, much to the surprise of Mahaprabhu's companions, who had not seen them together before. Without delay, Ramananda explained that the King, wishing to please Mahaprabhu, had released him from government service.

"By this generous act the King has served a devotee, and therefore pleased Krishna," said Mahaprabhu. "Krishna has said that a person devoted directly to him is not his devotee, whereas a person who serves his servant is the best devotee of all."

But still Mahaprabhu refused to meet King Prataparudra.

········

WORD CAME OF THE ARRIVAL of the devotees from Bengal. Mahaprabhu sent out Svarup and Govinda with garlands to greet them. From the roof of his palace, the King watched with Sarvabhauma as Govinda went forward to offer a garland to Advaita Acharya, whom Sarvabhauma identified as the leader of the devotees from Bengal, and a man honored even by Mahaprabhu. Seeing the visitors and hearing for the first time the sound of their singing made a deep impression upon the King.

"Never before have I heard the names of God chanted with such feeling," he marveled. "Nor have I seen such ecstatic love."

The devotees streamed into Mahaprabhu's residence, and he was overjoyed to see his beloved friends. He embraced Advaita and Shrivas, then each of them, one by one, as he welcomed them into Kashi Mishra's house. Once they were inside, he offered each one a garland and sandalwood paste to cool their foreheads.

Among them, one remained apart, lying in the road at a distance. This was Haridas Thakur, who, although revered by all present, felt himself unworthy to come any closer. The devotees begged him to come in, but he refused, saying he was unworthy to be so near the great temple of Jagannath.

"Let me have some solitary place nearby, a simple shelter where I can sit and chant."

Mahaprabhu heard of Haridas's desire and, seeing his humility, was moved with love for him.

"Here in the garden is a small cottage, secluded and quiet," he said to Kashi Mishra. "I want it for Haridas. Please give it to me."

Having acquired this boon, he sent everyone to bathe in the sea, while he went alone to meet Haridas. He found him sitting by the road happily chanting the holy name. Seeing Mahaprabhu approach, Haridasa bowed down before him, full length in the dusty road. Mahaprabhu raised him gently in his arms, and they embraced with great affection. Then Mahaprabhu led Haridas to the garden and showed him the cottage, which was surrounded by trees and flowering bushes.

"This room is for you. On Krishna's behalf you have undergone many trials in your life. Now you can stay near me and chant all day, every day. I will send you food, and from here you can see the pinnacle of Jagannath's temple."

Having accomplished this, Mahaprabhu joined the devotees on the beach. After bathing and eating, they visited the temple of Jagannath. There they danced and sang in four groups with Sri Krishna Chaitanya in their midst, leaping high into the air. As he danced, he cried profuse tears and his body shivered in ecstasy. Sometimes he fell to the ground and Nityananda picked him up. The devotees danced with abandon, each one thinking, "Mahaprabhu is looking only at me." No one could understand how this could be, yet all were certain it was so. As each of them came near him, he embraced them tightly, while tears of love flowed from his eyes. The King and all the people of Jagannath Puri watched this extraordinary spectacle and were amazed.

The Chariot Festival

The time of Rathayatra approached. The chariot festival, which had been held each year for as long as Jagannath had been worshipped, was the highlight of the devotees' lives, and attracted huge numbers of pilgrims. The name Jagannath, meaning "Lord of the Universe," referred to Krishna, who was worshipped together with his sister, Subhadra, and his brother, Balaram. Their three huge forms were carved from wood and each required many men to carry them. They were called *daru brahman*—spirit made of wood. Each summer, the three deities were lifted onto three enormous chariots and pulled in procession to the Gundicha temple, a mile away, where they stayed for a week before returning to the great temple. The procession commemorated the pilgrimage once taken by Krishna and his family to Kurukshetra; while there, Krishna had met his childhood friends, the people of Vrindavan, who had also come as pilgrims. The reunion between Krishna, then a prince of the Yadu dynasty, and his country cousins from the forest was an emotional one.

This festival of Rathayatra was an opportunity for all to see Jagannath and receive his loving gaze, just as the people of Vrindavan had done when Krishna went to Kurukshetra. On this one occasion of the year, anyone who saw Jagannath on his chariot was said to be liberated from the cycle of birth and death.

In preparation for Rathayatra, Mahaprabhu wanted to offer special service to Jagannath, so he asked permission to clean the Gundicha temple to make it ready for the arrival of Jagannath, Balaram, and Subhadra. The King granted his wish, and on the chosen day Mahaprabhu went to the Gundicha temple with hundreds of followers, each carrying a waterpot or a broom.

First, he led everyone in sweeping, beginning with the main altar and spreading out through the temple and kitchens, into the courtyard and all the way to the edges of the compound. Each of them tried to outdo the others in gathering the most leaves, twigs, and dust. When the temple and compound had been thoroughly swept, Mahaprabhu led the way in sweeping a second time so that even the tiniest particles of dust were collected. Only after this did they begin to wash the temple. Hundreds of pots of water were brought from the nearby lake and thrown over the ceilings, walls, and floors, beginning from the altar and working outward. With his own cloth, Mahaprabhu polished the altar and mopped the floors.

While they worked, they chanted "Hari!" and "Krishna! Krishna!" When the entire temple was thoroughly cleaned inside and out, it was fresh and cool, and the minds of the devotees felt as peaceful and purified as the temple. Mahaprabhu asked Svarup to start singing; as he sang, Mahaprabhu danced, his tears falling like raindrops. All joined him in carefree dancing and singing.

Afterward, they bathed in the lake and put on dry clothes. Then they sat in a nearby garden to enjoy a wonderful feast. Food was brought from the great Jagannath temple, enough to feed hundreds of people. Surrounded by joking and laughter, Mahaprabhu sat among the devotees with Sarvabhauma at his side.

"I used to spend my life debating with dry logicians," laughed Sarvabhauma. "Now I float in an ocean of friendship surrounded by loving friends."

"And in your company, Sarvabhauma, we are all learning to love Krishna," added Mahaprabhu.

·······

As was the custom during the two weeks before Rathayatra, Jagannath had been kept hidden from view. Now, on the eve of the festival, Jagannath could be seen again. Mahaprabhu had missed seeing his Lord, so he took a group of devotees with him and went to the great temple. They entered a side room and from there caught a private glimpse of Jagannath's beautiful form. They saw his large, red-rimmed eyes blossom like lotus flowers, his neck shine like a row of sapphires, and his broad smile spread as sweet as nectar. They were entranced; Mahaprabhu, his vision blurred by his own tears, could not take his gaze away from Jagannath's face.

The ceremony to bring the great deities out of the temple occurred the next morning. The three chariots waited on the road, each one having a broad platform supporting hundreds of attendants, borne upon sixteen gigantic wheels and covered by a red, yellow, or green canopy that towered fifty feet into the air. The sides of the wooden chariots were brightly painted, decorated with banners, bells, gongs, and mirrors; the canopies were topped by golden pinnacles sparkling in the morning sun, from which brightly colored flags fluttered in the sea breeze.

Powerfully built servants of Jagannath bound silken ropes around the waists of each deity and carried them out of the temple, following a pathway carpeted with thick cotton pillows. As they heaved the huge forms from one pad to the next, the pads burst, sending puffs of cotton wool floating into the air. As more pads were laid down, the King swept the way in front using a golden-handled broom. Thousands of onlookers pressed forward, singing and sounding all kinds of musical instruments. Mahaprabhu looked on with a loving gaze, repeating over and over, "Manima, Manima!," meaning "O great one!"

At the foot of each chariot a ramp had been constructed, upon which the deities were pulled until they stood upon their thrones high above the throng, surrounded by their attendant priests and servants. When everything was ready, with the sun already high in the sky, the procession began. Thick ropes were hauled by the crowd, and the chariots moved majestically. They creaked and swayed, through the broad main street of Jagannath Puri, surrounded by throngs of pilgrims. The procession moved slowly, sometimes halting, sometimes gaining speed, while thousands of adoring devotees sang and danced with abandon.

Mahaprabhu gathered his followers around him, applying cooling sandalwood paste to their foreheads and giving each one a flower garland. He formed them into seven *kirtan* groups, each with a lead singer, two drummers and a dancer. Then he arranged them around Jagannath's chariot and they started their ecstatic chanting. At first, he moved from one group to another, but then miraculously he was seen dancing in all seven groups at once. Each group thought, "Our merciful master is dancing just with us." In the same way that Krishna had danced with each *gopi* simultaneously in his circle dance of love, so Chaitanya Mahaprabhu danced among his devotees.

Mahaprabhu gazed into Jagannath's eyes as he danced in front of his chariot, with his devotees gathered around him in three circles to protect him from the crowd. As he moved, he appeared like a spinning circle of fire. Crying out the names of Krishna, he leaped high into the air, tears streaming from his eyes. Wherever he stepped, the earth seemed to tilt. One moment he stood motionless, his body shivering and pale; then his features reddened like a *mallika* flower, his hairs erupted on end, and tears shot from his eyes like torrents; the next moment, crying and trembling, he fell to the ground and rolled in the white sand; when this happened. Nityananda lifted him gently and held him tight. Such mystical signs of ecstasy had never before been seen.

Among those who witnessed Mahaprabhu's dancing in front of the Rathayatra cart, only Svarup understood its deeper significance. He knew it expressed Radha's longing to be with Krishna in the forest of Vrindavan. All year long, Jagannath lived in his grand temple with the Goddess of Fortune. Then, for just one week, he came out to journey with his devotees in the countryside. Jagannath's pilgrimage during Rathayatra evoked the occasion when Krishna, living as a prince in Dvaraka, left his royal city to meet his childhood friends from the forest. On that occasion, Radha came to meet her beloved Krishna. She was overjoyed to see him, yet she saw that, now he was a royal prince with royal wives, she would never again share with him the intimacy they had enjoyed in their youth in the forest of Vrindavan. The heartbreaking emotions felt by Radha overwhelmed Mahaprabhu as he danced in front of Jagannath.

"You are the same Krishna who stole my heart during my youth," he called out, "And I am the same Radha with the same intimate love. We are meeting on a moonlit night in spring, with the fragrance of *malati* flowers blowing through the *kadamba* trees, just as when we met in the beginning of our lives. Yet, although all this is the same, I long to be with you in the forest of Vrindavan beneath the *vetasi* tree on the bank of the Yamuna."

While Mahaprabhu sang this verse, he danced on and on; it seemed to his devotees that Jagannath, riding on the huge chariot, was spellbound watching him dance. While this scene unfolded, the procession reached wooded gardens appearing like Vrindavan on either side. Here was the place for the lunchtime stop. Thousands of devotees spread out under the trees and laid cloths upon the ground, preparing to make their midday offerings of food to Jagannath. Exhausted from his ecstatic dancing, Mahaprabhu lay in the shade of a tree and fell asleep upon the bare ground.

The King's Wish

All during the Rathayatra procession, the King had intently watched Mahaprabhu's wonderful dancing, but kept his distance so as not to disturb him. Now, encouraged by Sarvabhauma, he disguised himself as an ordinary devotee and entered the garden. There, he saw the figure of

Mahaprabhu sleeping.[17] Being careful not to disturb him, the King sat down at his feet and gently massaged them. As he did so, he sang softly of the *gopis'* love for Krishna, chanting Sanskrit verses from the *Srimad Bhagavatam*. The sound of these verses woke Mahaprabhu. He was captivated and urged the unknown singer to chant on. The King continued until he reached a particular verse sung to Krishna by the *gopis*.

"Your sweet words, chanted by great souls, give life to those who suffer in this world," he chanted. "The spiritual power of those words spreads everywhere to bless all who hear them, dissolving their burden of karma. The souls who chant these sweet words are the kindest of all."

When he heard these words, Mahaprabhu rose, exclaiming, "You are the kindest of all, for you have given me this wonderful gift."

Mahaprabhu repeated the verse again and again, until at length he asked his companion's name.

"I am the obedient follower of your devotees," replied the King. "I only wish to be the servant of your servants."

Mahaprabhu accepted the King's words. If he recognized him he did not say; instead he embraced his companion.

Seeing the King embraced by Mahaprabhu and at last achieving his blessings, everyone was happy. They understood that his good fortune was the result of his persistence and his humble approach. That very morning at the start of the Rathayatra, the King had swept the road in front of Jagannath's chariot. This humility had pleased Krishna, and so Mahaprabhu had accepted him; this, they said among themselves, was the secret of the King's success.

An elaborate feast with hundreds of varieties of food was liberally distributed, arranged by the King. Mahaprabhu took care to see that the many pilgrims who crowded around were included, and bid them chant the holy name of Hari. "Haribol!" they sang with delight.

All were tired from their exertions, but the afternoon was passing and the procession still had a distance to go before reaching the ancient temple of Gundicha. The crowd gathered around the chariots and although many hands were laid on the ropes, Jagannath's chariot would not move. Even though the King appointed his strongest men to pull the ropes, the chariot stood firm. Elephants were brought from the royal palace and harnessed to the chariot. Crying and bellowing, they strained at the ropes, but to everyone's surprise they could not advance a single step. An invisible force seemed to hold the chariot rooted to the spot.

Then an amazing thing happened. Mahaprabhu arrived with his followers and watched the elephants and heard their cries. He came forward, ordered them to be released, and asked his own devotees to hold the ropes. Then he pushed the chariot with his bare head. As if it had a life of its own, the great chariot rolled forward, rattling as it moved without the need of anyone pulling on the ropes. All who witnessed this were astonished. They sang the name of Mahaprabhu, calling him Gaurachandra, the Golden Moon. Ever after, they remembered this amazing feat—how he had made Jagannath's chariot move when no one else could.

By the end of the afternoon, the procession reached its destination, the spotlessly clean Gundicha temple. The deities were carried inside, once more offered food, and then ceremonially bathed and sung to sleep. Only then did Mahaprabhu and his companions retire for the night.

For the next week the deities of Jagannath, Balaram, and Subhadra remained at Gundicha, while Mahaprabhu stayed nearby with his devotees, singing and dancing each day. Sometimes he asked for particular songs to be sung while he danced alone beneath the trees, and sometimes he joined the others and they all danced and sang together. In the gardens surrounding the temple were two large lakes, called Indradyumna and Narendra. Diving into their cool waters, the devotees played, splashing and mock-fighting like children. Many were reminded of their childhood games with Nimai in the Ganges.

While he stayed at the Gundicha temple, Mahaprabhu immersed himself in the intimate mood of Vrindavan. Whereas at the great Jagannath temple the mood was of splendor and reverence for Jagannath as Master of the Universe, during this interlude of Rathayatra a more relaxed and spontaneous mood predominated. This was the spirit of Vrindavan, where Krishna is neither king nor master, but a youth among his beloved friends, who love him as much as life itself. Those friends saw him not as master of the universe, but as their beloved companion. Though Krishna lived as Jagannath in the magnificent Puri temple, he remembered those loving times in the forest when he played among his friends as equals, without formality or inhibition. Each year at Rathayatra he left behind his queen and royal palace, taking with him his brother, Balaram, and his sister, Subhadra, to seek the intimate company of his childhood friends.

Mahaprabhu asked Svarup to explain why the natural beauty of Vrindavan attracted Krishna so.

"The land of Vrindavan is made of touchstone and crystals," sang Svarup. "It is a forest of desire trees whose fruits and flowers grant the inhabitants all their wishes. The cows grazing among those trees supply unlimited milk and the water tastes like nectar. The cowherd girls living there are more beautiful than the Goddess of Fortune—their voices are like music, their graceful movements are like dancing, and their constant companion is the sound of Krishna's flute."

Shrivas heard these words and laughed. His devotion belonged to the Goddess of Fortune in Krishna's royal palace, where more reverential feelings for Krishna abounded. He and Svarup exchanged opinions about their spiritual preferences, and their discussion delighted all who heard it. Each of the devotees of Krishna had their own way to express their love; some reverential, some playful, some with heartfelt emotion—each in accord with their particular spiritual nature.

Throughout his life, Mahaprabhu emphasized this intimate mood of Vrindavan, and especially during Rathayatra week, which became the climax of the year for his followers. From as far away as Bengal they came to share with him the sweet mood of Vrindavan.

On the ninth day, the festivities drew to a close and a great procession rolled its way back to the main temple of Jagannath Puri, carrying the deities on their chariots. So the magic of that week passed, and Jagannath returned to his palace for another year.

Return to Bengal

The time came for the devotees from Bengal to return home. Before they left, Mahaprabhu called them together for special instructions. First he spoke with Nityananda. Though they were not related by birth, Mahaprabhu always called Nityananda his older brother, while Nityananda called Mahaprabhu his master, and dedicated himself to encouraging others to serve him.

"I need you to stay in Bengal to lead my mission," said Mahaprabhu to Nityananda. "I see no one else who can succeed at this difficult task. Take with you some trusted helpers and give everyone the gift of devotion to Krishna." Following this appeal, Nityananda became the charismatic leader of the devotees in Bengal, tirelessly traveling about the country to spread love of God.[18]

Then Mahaprabhu spoke to Advaita, asking him to teach Krishna devotion among the less fortunate. Advaita felt a special concern for those outside the higher castes; Mahaprabhu asked him to give them the same chance as others to enter the path of Krishna consciousness.

Someone asked how a householder should practice spiritual life.

"Always chant the name of Krishna and serve the Vaishnavas," Mahaprabhu instructed.

"How should I recognize a true Vaishnava?"

"Whoever chants Krishna's name even once is to be honored as the best of persons," he said. "No other spiritual practice is necessary. Krishna's name frees the soul from material conditioning, dissolves all obstacles on the spiritual path, and awakens the soul's natural love for Krishna. Anyone who ceaselessly chants Krishna's name is to be honored as a Vaishnava."

"And among Vaishnavas," he continued, "The one whose mere presence inspires others to chant Krishna's name is the best of all."

One by one, Mahaprabhu said farewell to the devotees, giving each one personal encouragement. Inspired by his instructions, they left for the journey home, contemplating how they would help Nityananda fulfill the mission he had been given.

········

WHEN NITYANANDA GOT BACK TO BENGAL, he gave up his former austere ways and found a new freedom. He took to wearing brightly colored clothes and multi-colored silk turbans, with long flower garlands, pearl necklaces, earrings, bracelets, and gold rings. His exuberance complemented Mahaprabhu's simplicity and attracted many bright, young followers. Among them were singers, dancers, and musicians. When they sang and danced together, with Nityananda in their midst, they spread joy around them. Since Mahaprabhu had gone to Puri, the people of Navadvip felt they had lost their dearest companion; now they came to life again, inspired by Nityananda.

He went to Sachi's house. She had not recovered from the loss of her divine son, but now she found new hope, feeling he had returned in the form of his spiritual brother, Nityananda. She begged him to stay nearby and he agreed to her request, making Navadvip his headquarters. From there, he traveled throughout Bengal to spread Mahaprabhu's *sankirtan* movement.

So it was that although Mahaprabhu now lived in Puri, his movement continued to grow in Bengal through the dedication of Nityananda, who showed special concern for those who had fallen to the bottom of society; the very poorest who had to struggle to feed themselves; the outcasts; even the criminals; all were touched by his friendship and generosity. Navadvip became a charmed city, where even the vagabonds and thieves reformed to become devotees of Krishna.

Nityananda also influenced the Muslim rulers. The local Kazi was unrelenting in his opposition to the Hindu chanting. He feared it would stir up sectarian feelings at a time when Bengal's Muslim rulers were at war with the neighboring Hindu state of Orissa. One day, a follower of Nityananda, Gadadhar Das, fearlessly begged the Kazi to chant the name of Hari. He dismissed Gadadhar's direct appeal.

"Go home, Gadadhar. Tomorrow I will chant Hari," he said in a light-hearted mood. Gadadhar clapped his hands with joy.

"Now you have chanted the name of Hari, your sins have vanished," he cried. In such ways, Muslims were influenced to chant Krishna's names and the spirit of the *sankirtan* movement was spread by Nityananda and his band of chanting devotees.

········

TWO MORE YEARS PASSED. Mahaprabhu was happy in Puri, but longed to travel to Vrindavan to see Krishna's home. Ever since meeting his spiritual master in Gaya he had intended to go, but there had been delays. First, he had returned to his family and established the path of devotion to Krishna among his own people in Navadvip; then when he became a *sannyasi*, to please his mother he had moved to Jagannath Puri instead of Vrindavan; then for two years he had traveled in South India, preaching as a *sannyasi*. Now, four years after he left Navadvip, the journey to Vrindavan was always in his thoughts.

When Rathayatra was over for the third year, Mahaprabhu told his companions he wanted to visit Krishna's homeland. Previously, when he had mentioned this, they had not wanted him to go, partly because the journey was hazardous and partly because they were frightened of losing him. This time, however, they gave way.

"If you must go, please wait for the rains to end," they said. "Then it will be easier for you to travel."

Three months later, when the day of Vijaya Dasami arrived, commemorating the victory of Rama over Ravana and marking the change of season, Mahaprabhu set out. His plan was first to travel north along the coast as far as Bengal, where he would visit his mother and bathe in the Ganges at

Navadvip. Then he would follow the course of the Ganges and Yamuna Rivers westward until he reached Vrindavan.

He set off with a large company of devotees. The first part of his journey brought him to Bhubaneshwar, capital of Orissa, full of ornate temples. Here he was met by King Prataparudra, who made elaborate arrangements for his onward journey, ordering resthouses to be prepared at stopping places along the way, and assigning a bodyguard to travel with the group. Where Mahaprabhu was to cross the great River Mahanadi, the King ordered them to mark the spot for posterity.

"I will come there to bathe," he declared, "and I may also die there."

Together with his queens, the King gave Mahaprabhu a royal send-off. In easy stages the party reached the northern borders of Orissa, where the Bay of Bengal meets the mouth of the Ganga. This was the limit of the King's authority, and here his officers and bodyguards prepared to say farewell. Beyond lay hostile country, patrolled by guards loyal to Nawab Hussein Shah, the Muslim ruler of Bengal. The Nawab was at war with Orissa and had already destroyed many Hindu temples. To guarantee Mahaprabhu's safe onward passage, the King's officers had to first negotiate with their Muslim counterparts. There was a delay of a few days while messages passed back and forth; then, to everyone's surprise, Hussein Shah himself arrived to see Mahaprabhu. The Nawab's curiosity had been aroused by reports that had reached him, and when he met Mahaprabhu in person he was genuinely moved by his spirituality. The Muslim ruler offered his personal help, providing boats and guards to take the party into the waters of the Ganges delta.

As they embarked, Mahaprabhu spoke with Gadadhar, who had insisted on coming because he could not bear to be left behind.

"Your service to Krishna lies in Puri, my dear Gadadhar. That is where you belong. I will soon return." Gadadhar protested with tears in his eyes, but Mahaprabhu was firm.

"You cannot come with me."

As he watched the boats pull away, Gadadhar remained on the riverbank in tears, while Mahaprabhu, his boat moving swiftly into the stream, looked steadfastly away.

Mahaprabhu and his party were carried safely up into the mouths of the Ganges, protected by the Nawab's guards from the pirates who haunted those waters. Journeying along wide, palm-thronged channels, they passed upstream deep into Bengal as far as Panihati on the edge of the district of Nadia.

So it was that, four years after his departure as a lone *sannyasi*, Sri Krishna Chaitanya reentered his homeland with a government escort, unannounced, to the surprise and joy of his Bengali devotees.

For three weeks, Mahaprabhu moved from house to house, staying with Shrivas, Shivananda Sen, and Vidya Vachaspati, the brother of Sarvabhauma. Word of his arrival spread; wherever he went he was besieged by crowds of eager devotees. At Vidya Vachaspati's home near Navadvip, the crowds overran the surrounding countryside. So many tried to cross the Ganges to see him that the river was thick with people, desperate by any means just to get a glimpse of him. Some of the overladen boats capsized, yet no one perished. Seeing the vast numbers, and not wanting to endanger lives, Mahaprabhu slipped away in the middle of the night to another part of Navadvip. When dawn came and people discovered he had left, they searched for him again and soon found him at another house. This time, he showed himself to the crowds, and the air resounded with the sound of Krishna's names. When he saw the vast numbers and heard their thunderous *kirtan*, he wept. He and Nityananda joined in the *sankirtan*, dancing in ecstasy. All who witnessed these events felt themselves blissfully transformed, freed forever from the bonds of birth and death by the outpouring of Mahaprabhu's divine love.

He eventually came to Advaita Acharya's house in Shantipur. There his mother was at last able to be with him and gain some relief from her pain of separation. After staying for some days, he set off on the road to Vrindavan.

He traveled amid a great crowd of followers. As they passed through fields and villages, more people flocked to join them. With Mahaprabhu were Haridas and others who had started out with him from Puri. They were joined by many more devotees from Navadvip, led by Nityananda, Shrivas, Mukunda, and Murari. All were intent on accompanying him all the way to Vrindavan. The party followed the main roads from village to village along the Ganges, their numbers growing ever larger. As they passed through the countryside, people took dust from the ground marked by Mahaprabhu's footprints, leaving holes in the road. So he reached the village of Ramakeli, which stood on the bank of the Ganges close to Gauda, the capital of Bengal.

Here lived two gifted brothers who had risen to become youthful ministers in the government of Nawab Hussein Shah. They came from a high-caste *brahmana* family originating in South India, but had renounced their *brahmana* status to accept service in the Muslim government. Their learning and intelligence, and the high esteem in which they were held by the people, made them much valued by the Nawab. Despite their youth—they were in their late twenties—the Nawab made them his closest advisers, one being his Finance Minister and the other his Private Secretary. Secretly, however, they were devotees of Krishna, and for some time they had been corresponding with Mahaprabhu, professing their devotion to him.

In the night, hidden from prying eyes, the two brothers came to see their master. They bowed full length on the ground and tearfully offered him their prayers.

"We feel ashamed to come before you because we are sinful. But we know that you are the savior of Jagai and Madhai, and you have come to save fallen people like us. Apart from you, no one can rescue us from our degraded condition. We are like dwarfs who want to catch the moon—we aspire for your mercy. Please allow us to serve you."

Mahaprabhu was moved to hear these humble words.

"Please arise and don't speak like this anymore," he said. "I know your hearts are full of love for Krishna, for I have read your letters. Did you not receive my reply? I wrote, 'A woman with a secret lover may appear busy serving her husband, but in her heart she thinks always of her lover.'" So saying he laid his hands on their heads.

"People may wonder why I came here. They do not know it was just to see you two. I give you the names Rupa and Sanatan. You are my eternal servants, and have been so through many births. Do not fear, Krishna will soon release you from your entanglement." Then he embraced them, and the devotees present rejoiced, giving the two brothers their blessings.

Rupa and Sanatan hurried away, but before leaving, Sanatan had some advice for his new master. He was worried that Mahaprabhu would attract unwelcome attention, particularly from Hussein Shah and his Muslim deputies. The Nawab had offered his protection, but Sanatan feared he might change his mind when he saw the size of the crowds that followed Mahaprabhu. His advice was to not travel so conspicuously. In his opinion it would be better for a *sannyasi* to travel to Vrindavan alone without drawing attention to himself.

After considering Sanatana's advice, Mahaprabhu decided he must abandon his journey to Vrindavan, return to Jagannath Puri, and make a separate pilgrimage later on. So, having reached Ramakeli and blessing Rupa and Sanatan, Mahaprabhu returned the way he had come.

·······

While Mahaprabhu was traveling back through Bengal, a young man came to see him. This was Raghunath, whose father was a wealthy benefactor of the Vaishnavas and a close friend of Advaita's. Four years earlier, when Sri Krishna Chaitanya had stayed at Advaita's house after becoming a *sannyasi*, the youthful Raghunath had been allowed to serve him. Mahaprabhu had placed his feet on Raghunath's head, and the youth had been so affected that he wanted to leave everything and accompany Mahaprabhu at once to Jagannath Puri; but his father had forbidden him. Since then, Raghunath had stayed at home thinking only of when he could renounce family life and go to Puri. His father wanted him to settle down and look after the family business. He arranged a marriage for him with a beautiful young girl, did everything he could to make home life comfortable, and set guards to watch over him day and night. Raghunath felt trapped.

Now the young man heard that Mahaprabhu was again staying with Advaita, and begged his father's leave to go there. His father reluctantly agreed, sending a party of servants to keep a close watch over him, and making him promise to return within a week. So Raghunath came to Advaita's house, where Mahaprabhu was staying in Shantipur. When Mahaprabhu saw Raghunath, he knew his mind was full of thoughts of escaping to Jagannath Puri. He spoke to him lovingly but firmly.

"Krishna will soon deliver you from the ocean of material life," he told Raghunath. "Until then you should return home and live normally. Enjoy what Krishna has given you, without allowing yourself to be attached. When the time is right, in a year or two, when I have completed my pilgrimage to Vrindavan, then you can come and join me in Puri. Krishna will show you how."

Raghunath was encouraged by these words and returned home with a peaceful heart. His parents, seeing the change in him, relaxed their guard. So he lived at home for a while longer, behaving as a responsible married man and patiently waiting for Krishna to release him. Later, as foretold by Mahaprabhu, he gained his freedom and came to stay with his master in Puri, where he renounced his former wealth and lived by begging, always absorbed in continual prayer and meditation upon Radha and Krishna.

For seven days, Mahaprabhu stayed with Advaita, and his mother came to cook for him. This was the last time mother and son were together in this life, and their eventual parting was full of sorrow.

Quietly taking his leave, Mahaprabhu traveled back to Puri with only a few companions. He had been away for eight months; he had given his love to many thousands in Bengal, initiated two young men destined to be among his most influential disciples, and encouraged Raghunath; but he had failed to reach Vrindavan. Once back in Puri he urgently resumed preparations for his pilgrimage.

Pilgrimage to Vrindavan

At the end of the rainy season just before dawn, a few months after he had returned from Bengal, Mahaprabhu slipped away unnoticed from the city of Jagannath Puri. Ahead of him lay the wild jungle.

When he arrived back in Puri he told his companions of how he had turned back before reaching Vrindavan. Krishna had not wanted it, he had said; so many people had followed him, and it was impossible to continue.

"Dear Gadadhar, Krishna was not happy that I left you behind," he said, taking Gadadhar's hand. "That is why he stopped me from reaching my destination."

But he had succeeded in meeting Rupa and Sanatan. He described these two special persons, and how their learning and humility made a deep impression upon him.

"They said I should go to Vrindavan alone. Now I ask you all to help me try again."

His friends agreed; Mahaprabhu would stay in Puri for the rainy season, then leave for Vrindavan with one companion. It was important that this companion should not provoke the envy of those left behind, so a quiet and capable *brahmana*, Balabhadra Bhattacharya, was chosen. He was a scholar and a good cook, and he would take with him an assistant to help him look after his master as they traveled.

The trio set off early one morning, their path leading away from the main road, through wild places where humans rarely ventured. They passed elephants, tigers, boar, and rhinoceros. Mahaprabhu's companions were afraid, but the animals seemed under a spell and moved aside without harming them. One day, a tiger lay in their path and Mahaprabhu touched it with his foot. Springing to its feet, the tiger danced and called the name of Krishna. Another time they had reached a river where Mahaprabhu sat in meditation, when a herd of elephants emerged from the forest and silently stared at him. He splashed them playfully and commanded, "Chant Krishna!" They swayed their ponderous heads with pleasure, trumpeting Krishna's names.

As he walked, Mahaprabhu constantly chanted. Attracted by his sweet voice, deer silently followed behind, while peacocks and other birds flew overhead, responding with Krishna's names. In his presence, animals who were natural enemies became friends and the weak no longer feared the strong. All creatures felt his love and danced joyfully together.

Wild roots and vegetables were plentiful in the forest; Balabhadra was expert at collecting ingredients for their meals. In the villages along the way people gave them rice and Mahaprabhu taught them to chant the holy name. Whoever heard him chant would teach another, who taught a third, and so, as he walked through the forest chanting Krishna's names in great happiness, the chanting spread. After a month they had crossed the range of hills bordering northeast Orissa and reached their halfway point, Varanasi on the banks of the Ganges. This was North India's greatest center of pilgrimage and learning.

Here waited the pious Tapan Mishra. When Mahaprabhu had toured East Bengal ten years earlier as a young householder, he had met Tapan Mishra and asked him to move to Varanasi, promising they would meet again. Since then, Tapan Mishra had lived here with his family, patiently waiting for his master to fulfill his word.[19] One day he came to the Ganges to bathe and saw Mahaprabhu there beside the water's edge. With a cry he ran forward to catch his master's feet. They embraced and Tapan Mishra took Mahaprabhu to his home, where he fed him and made him comfortable. Then he went to find his friend Chandrashekhar. The two of them shared a deep faith in Krishna.

The leading teacher of Varanasi was a *sannyasi* named Prakashananda. He had heard from friends in Puri of the young *sannyasi* Sri Krishna Chaitanya, but held no regard for a renunciant who spent his time singing and dancing and attracting sentimental followers. When he heard that Mahaprabhu was in Varanasi, he laughed aloud.

Tapan Mishra and Chandrashekhar, deeply upset by Prakashananda's ridicule, hurried to tell Mahaprabhu, but he only smiled. For now he was intent on going to Vrindavan. Later, he would return to meet Prakashananda and his followers.

For ten days, Mahaprabhu stayed at Tapan Mishra's home in Varanasi. Then, promising to return, he continued on his way to Vrindavan with his two companions. Reaching the confluence of the Ganges and Yamuna at Prayag, they stayed for three days to bathe in the holy waters. Here their route joined the Yamuna River, so dear to Krishna, and Mahaprabhu's ecstasy deepened. Their path lay along her bank. As before, Mahaprabhu taught many along the way to chant Krishna's names and spread his message of love for God.

At last they reached Mathura, birthplace of Krishna. They met a *brahmana* disciple of Madhavendra Puri. Although Madhavendra's name was not widely known, he had been an elevated devotee of Radha and Krishna, who had initiated his followers into the secret wisdom of *madhurya-rasa*, the sweet love of the soul for Krishna in the mood of lover and beloved. His disciples included Advaita Acharya, Nityananda, and Mahaprabhu's own master, Ishvara Puri. Mahaprabhu revered Madhavendra Puri as his grand-preceptor and was very pleased to meet his disciple. So he stayed in the *brahmana*'s home.

After seeing Krishna's birthplace in Mathura, Mahaprabhu traveled through the twelve forests of Vrindavan. The forests were remote and sparsely populated places, filled with abundant wildlife. Entering this paradise, he was transported to another world. Cows licked his feet; deer heard his sweet voice and flocked around him; parrots, cuckoos, and bees hovered about his head; trees and creepers blossomed in his presence and bent their branches, laden with fruits, to touch his feet. The whole forest came alive, as if all living things recognized that Krishna had returned among them.

Embracing the deer, he constantly chanted "Krishna, Krishna." The sight of blue-throated peacocks made him faint, for in the cries of peacocks and the chirping of green parrots he heard the names of Radha and Krishna. Whatever ecstasy he had felt in Puri increased ever more as he wandered the land of Vrindavan.

He came to Govardhan Hill, once lifted by Krishna's hand. Beside the hill were the two ponds where Krishna and Radha used to meet and bathe. These ponds had been forgotten; people no longer knew what they were. He identified them as special to Krishna's memory and reestablished them as sacred places. They were later extended to become large stone-lined tanks where pilgrims bathed and said their prayers to Radha and Krishna.

Mahaprabhu stayed beside Govardhan Hill for many days. Seeing the hill's beauty, he sang a verse from the *Srimad Bhagavatam*: "Govardhan Hill is the dearest servant of the Lord! Touched by his lotus feet, it joyfully gives fresh water, soft grass, edible roots, vegetables, and sheltering caves to serve Krishna and Balaram, and their friends and cows."

He continued through the twelve forests of Vrindavan, until he came to the banks of the Yamuna River. Here, where Krishna danced with the *gopis*, Mahaprabhu stayed for several weeks. Autumn turned to winter, and the Yamuna's waters grew cold and covered with mist. Mahaprabhu sat in the pale morning sun beneath an *amli* tree, at a place called Amlitala. From this spot he looked out at the Yamuna while chanting Krishna's names. In the afternoon, when people gathered around, he taught them to chant.

As news of the pure-hearted young *sannyasi* spread, people flocked to see him. As the crowds grew, Balabhadra Bhattacharya found them difficult to handle. He had faithfully cared for Mahaprabhu ever since they had left Puri. In his view, Mahaprabhu had done what he set out to do: he had seen Vrindavan and visited the holy places more or less alone and undisturbed. Now, the longer he stayed, the more unwelcome attention he would attract. So Balabhadra decided it was time to leave Vrindavan and return to Puri.

In the short days of winter, traveling with a party of three, Chaitanya Mahaprabhu walked south along the Yamuna, then east along the path beside the river in the direction of Prayag and Varanasi. He had achieved his life's ambition to visit Krishna's home, but he still had important tasks to accomplish before his pilgrimage was complete.

Teaching Rupa and Sanatan

After their late-night talks with Mahaprabhu in Ramakeli, the two brothers Rupa and Sanatan had returned to their official duties. Their experience of meeting Krishna Chaitanya face-to-face filled them with a new sense of purpose. Enough of their lives had been given to worldly affairs; they both felt the time had come for radical change. Sanatan lost interest in his official work, and instead began staying at home. There he surrounded himself with learned scholars of scripture. Wishing to make up for lost time, he immersed himself in hearing and studying the great holy book of Vaishnavism, *Srimad Bhagavatam*.

However, the two brothers were important members of the government of Nawab Hussein Shah, the powerful and feared ruler of Bengal. He had no intention of losing them, especially Sanatan, who was his Finance Minister. Without them, who would run his government while he was away on military campaigns? One day, he arrived without warning on Sanatan's doorstep, demanding to know why he seemed to be avoiding his work. When he learned that Sanatan wanted to retire, the ruler was outraged. He had affection for Sanatan and treated him almost like a brother, but his mood could quickly change when he was displeased. He ordered Sanatan to be kept under the vigilance of an armed guard until his return; then he left to pursue other business.

Meanwhile, Rupa had heard about Mahaprabhu's second journey to Vrindavan, this time traveling alone. Hastily concluding his affairs, Rupa set out with his younger brother, Anupam, intending to meet Mahaprabhu in Krishna's holy land. Before leaving, he deposited ten thousand gold coins in the care of a trusted local merchant, along with a message for Sanatan to use the money to buy his freedom and join them in Vrindavan as soon as possible.

········

EARLY IN THE YEAR 1516, Mahaprabhu was on his way back from Vrindavan, walking along the path by the Yamuna. As he walked he thought of Rupa and Sanatan. He knew from the moment he met them that they would be the ones he could entrust his message to; with their learning and experience of the world, with their pure hearts and humility, they could understand him and pass on his teachings for succeeding generations. He had important things to teach them and hoped to meet them again soon. He again reached the confluence of the Ganges and Yamuna at Prayag and decided to halt there so he could bathe in the sacred waters during the great winter festival of Magh Mela. Here, outside the temple of Madhava, he met Rupa and Anupam. From a distance they saw one another, the two brothers humbly bowing to him and the effulgent golden *sannyasi*, surrounded by an adoring crowd, hastening over to them.

"I bow before Krishna in his golden form of Sri Krishna Chaitanya," prayed Rupa, reciting a Sanskrit verse he had composed. "You are kindest of all, for you bring the gift of Krishna-*prema*, pure love for Krishna, to one and all."

Mahaprabhu embraced them both with great happiness, assuring them that Krishna had freed them forever from the prison of material life.

Now he would enlighten Rupa with the secrets of Krishna consciousness. Some days passed before an opportunity arose. They arranged to meet just outside the town, at the Dashashvamedha bathing *ghat*. There, over a period of ten days, Mahaprabhu taught Rupa about Krishna, about service to Krishna, and about the intricate secrets of loving relationships between Krishna and his devotees. He began by describing the truth about Krishna and his creation.

⌣ *Teachings* ⌢

"This universe is filled with numberless living beings, who are tiny sparks of the Supreme Spirit. They migrate from one species to another, from one planet to another, in a cycle of rebirth that has been going on since time began. Some live as immobile entities, such as plants or stones, while others move in the sea, in the air, or over the land. Among those moving on the land, humans are very few, and civilized humans fewer still. Of all these, the ones who have no desire other than to serve Krishna are rare.

"Such compassionate devotees of Krishna live in this world only to enlighten lost souls and pass on the seed of love for Krishna. If by the mercy of a servant of Krishna you receive the seed of devotion, then sow it in the garden of your heart. Water the seed by chanting Krishna's holy names or talking about Krishna with his devotees. From it will grow the creeper of devotion. Continue to water that creeper and it will climb beyond this universe to enter the spiritual world, where it will embrace the desire tree of Krishna's lotus feet and put forth fruits of divine love.

"The gardener must beware the great enemy of devotion—to harbor mistrust toward compassionate servants of Krishna. Such mistrust invites the mad elephant of envy into the garden of the heart and risks destroying everything. Regular chanting of Krishna's name, with faith and humility, nourishes and protects the creeper of devotion from this danger and from other obstacles to love, such as violence, greed, pride, the lure of mystic powers, and the last snare of illusion: the desire to be God. All such desires hinder the appearance of pure devotion. A pure devotee desires only the service of Krishna.

"A soul who enters the path of constant service to Krishna becomes attached to him, and this attachment soon turns to prema—love for God. As liquid sugarcane juice is refined into molasses, then sugar, *then pure crystals, so attachment to Krishna matures over time until it becomes intense ecstatic love for the Lord.*

"*Attachment for Krishna has five stages named* santa, dasya, sakhya, vatsalya, *and* madhurya; *these are: passive appreciation of Krishna's greatness; dependence on Krishna as his everlasting servant; love for Krishna as a friend; caring for Krishna as a child; and love for Krishna as a lover.*

"*When passive appreciation of Krishna's greatness increases in reverence, it grows into service; when service becomes more intimate, it turns into friendship; when friendship increases in affection and caring for the Lord, it becomes parental love; and when all these feelings increase in intimacy, conjugal love arises. Conjugal love is the culmination of all other relationships.*"

For ten days, Mahaprabhu expanded on these topics, teaching Rupa everything about pure love for Krishna.

"Always think of Krishna," he concluded. "Then Krishna will manifest in your heart and reveal everything to you."

With these words, Mahaprabhu ended his teachings to Rupa. He asked Rupa to write down all he had heard, and in this way to describe the secrets of *bhakti-rasa*, the deep and varied spiritual emotions of devotional service to Krishna. Then he embraced Rupa and told him to go to Vrindavan. Rupa desperately wanted to go with his master to Jagannath Puri, but now was not to be the time. Later, Mahaprabhu told him, he could come and visit him there.

With these words, Mahaprabhu boarded a boat, leaving Rupa standing on the shore, watching his master slip downstream toward Varanasi. Rupa's grief was so intense that he fainted and had to be helped to his lodgings. The next day, he and Anupam left for Vrindavan.

As his boat glided away, Mahaprabhu did not look back. His thoughts were on Rupa's brother Sanatan, for whom he also had a special mission, and on the philosophers of Varanasi. Soon he would meet them all, show them his friendship and speak to them about Krishna. A few days later, he arrived at Varanasi, where he was met outside the town by his loyal servants Chandrashekhar and Tapan Mishra. They led him and his attendants to their homes, where they were looked after with great care. Mahaprabhu stayed with Chandrashekhar and his attendants stayed with Tapan Mishra.

········

In Bengal, Sanatan had been under house arrest. Fortunately, the trusted merchant had managed to deliver Rupa's message along with the gold coins. Sanatan lost no time in buying his freedom, advising the head guard to say he had drowned himself in the Ganges.

"Have no fear," he assured the guard. "No one will see me here again: I will retire from the world and travel to Mecca." Which was more or less the truth, for as soon as Sanatan had been helped across the river, he disappeared into the hills, traveling by wild country tracks in the direction of Varanasi. Passersby saw only a poor mendicant dressed in torn clothes, carrying no possessions. The winter nights were cold, but Sanatan was happy to be free at last to give himself to the service of Mahaprabhu. On the road he met his wealthy brother-in-law, Shrikant, who promised secrecy and gave him a fine woolen shawl to keep him warm.

After traveling for two weeks, Sanatan arrived in Varanasi, just at the time that Mahaprabhu himself was there. Hearing of his master's presence, Sanatan made his way to the house where Mahaprabhu was staying. There, he sat on the ground outside and waited patiently.

········

In the morning at Chandrashekhar's house, Mahaprabhu spoke to his host: "Go outside and see if there is a Vaishnava at your door."

Chandrashekhar looked in front of his house and saw only what appeared to be an unshaven Muslim mendicant sitting nearby. Returning, he reported that no Vaishnava was there.

"Look again, and whoever is there, bring him to me," ordered Mahaprabhu. So Chandrashekhar called the mendicant into his courtyard, and Mahaprabhu at once ran out to embrace him. Reunited again, the two looked at each other with deep emotion. Then Sanatan pulled away: "Please do not hold me, Lord, I am not worthy of your touch."

"On the contrary, I am purified by touching you," said Mahaprabhu. "Because you always remember Krishna you are yourself a holy shrine, and just to see you, touch you, or speak of you is my perfection. Believe me, those whom the world honors but who do not serve Krishna, are not so good as the least of those devoted to the Lord."

They sat down and Mahaprabhu made Sanatan tell him everything about his escape from the Nawab. Then he sent him with Chandrashekhar to bathe and dress in clean clothes. Sanatan put on simple Vaishnava robes, but he refused the new cloth Chandrashekhar offered him. He would not take anything new or fine to wear because he wanted to relinquish all unnecessary comforts. He even gave his fine woolen shawl to a pilgrim in exchange for an old torn piece of cloth.

When Mahaprabhu saw this, he was filled with love for Sanatan, and resolved to teach him all about Krishna and the art of service to Krishna, up to the highest stages of divine love.

"I have fallen into the well of material enjoyment," submitted Sanatan. "People may think me wise, but in truth I know nothing. Now you have rescued me, so please teach me. Who am I? Why do I suffer in this world? How can I be healed? Be merciful and show me the truth." Being so asked, Mahaprabhu revealed his secret teachings to Sanatan in terms of three topics: the soul's relationship to Krishna; how to revive that eternal relationship; and the ultimate goal of life.

⌇ *Teachings* ⌇

"The nature of the soul is to be the eternal servant of Krishna," Mahaprabhu began. *"Krishna's potencies are three: spirit, matter, and soul. The innumerable souls by nature belong to spirit, but they have the freedom to choose matter. Those souls who choose to turn away from Krishna and live in the worlds of matter are enveloped by fear and illusion. The only escape from this fear is to seek Krishna's shelter. Krishna has the power to dispel the illusion, for he created it. Krishna guides the souls in this world, through holy books and teachers, reminding them of their eternal relationship with God, ultimately leading them to discover Krishna as that Supreme Person.*

"Now I will speak about the soul's relationship with Krishna.

"Krishna lives everywhere in his creation. Whatever you experience comes from Krishna. He expands himself into innumerable divine forms, all equivalent to his original form of Godhead, as innumerable candles lit from one candle are of equal power to that original candle. These multiple forms of God pervade all life and stand guardian over us in all directions, at all times, as protector, father, mother, and friend. They are described in the Vedic scriptures, and include the many avatars of Vishnu who come into this world to teach, inspire, protect, and show love to the living beings.

"Krishna reveals his personal beauty and love as he journeys through the countless worlds of matter he creates. He shows himself and his deeds throughout the worlds, just as the sun illuminates the far-flung corners of this globe—somewhere rising, somewhere setting, and somewhere standing at noon. Thus the soul has partial sight of Krishna in this world, like a glimpse of the moon caught among the branches of a tree.

"Krishna's spiritual potency spreads like an endless luminous sky filled with effulgent planets more numerous than the atoms in this universe. These eternal planets cluster like lotus petals about the whorl of Krishna's personal home, Goloka Vrindavan." As Mahaprabhu spoke, his ecstasy overflowed; he sang verses from the Bhagavatam in praise of Krishna's beauty.

"Krishna appears in this world as a rain cloud appears in the sky, his necklace of pearls is like a row of white ducks, his peacock feather is like a rainbow, his yellow garments flash like lightning. His sweet pastimes shower upon us like rain falling upon the fields.

"Unable to see enough of Krishna's beauty, the girls in the forest prayed, 'How inconsiderate is the creator! When we wish for thousands of eyes to see Krishna's beauty, he gave us only two eyes, and they keep blinking, preventing us from tasting Krishna's sweetness at every second.'

"Krishna's potencies are like the limitless ocean. My words can touch only a drop of them."

· · · · · · ·

Having explained the soul's relationship to Krishna, Mahaprabhu then taught Sanatan how to revive that eternal relationship.

Most souls are forever free in the eternal realm of the spirit; only some choose to turn away from Krishna and so descend into this world where they become bound by matter. In pursuit of their desires they enter material bodies and wander in the cycle of birth and death, passing through countless lifetimes suffering the pains of mortal life. If they are fortunate, such souls meet a holy teacher, one who can free them from the bonds of birth and death. This freedom is found through the path of service to God, by giving oneself to Krishna in love.

"You can give yourself to Krishna in six ways. Accept what is favorable to his service; avoid what is unfavorable to his service; believe in his protection; be confident he will maintain you; depend on his will; and practice humility.

"Service to Krishna begins with finding a teacher. Even a moment in the company of a pure devotee of Krishna is enough to bring you success. Under the guidance of a teacher, practice devotional service. The five key principles of devotional service are: associate with devotees; chant the names of God; hear or read about Krishna in holy scriptures such as Srimad Bhagavatam; *live in Vrindavan or near a temple of Krishna; and worship the deity of Krishna.*

"Pure love for Krishna lives in the heart of every being. When your heart is purified by service, love awakens naturally.

"In this awakened state you can offer your love to Krishna in everything you do: in hearing, chanting, remembering, worshipping, praying, serving, and obeying, in friendship, or in surrendering everything to him. Most important among these nine are the first three: hearing, chanting, and remembering. They are the beginning of devotion.

"When love awakens, a lover of God is no longer bound by any rule, and service becomes spontaneous. At this point Krishna's devotee is attracted to remember a particular companion of Krishna in Vrindavan and to follow in the footsteps of that spiritual guide, meditating with deep absorption upon the service offered to Krishna by that divine person."

········

After Mahaprabhu had outlined the path to reviving the soul's eternal relationship with Krishna, he went on to describe life's ultimate goal: love of God.

"When affection for Krishna deepens to love, it shines like the sun and softens the heart with spiritual emotions. The symptoms of one who is in love with Krishna are forgiveness, careful use of time, detachment, humility, hope, eagerness, attraction to chanting Krishna's names, attachment to hearing about Krishna, and affection for the holy places associated with Krishna.

"In this stage of pure love a person laughs, cries, and calls upon

Krishna's name without caring for public opinion. Being absorbed in love for Krishna in one of the five primary rasas, *or relationships, such that a devotee experiences waves of ecstasy stimulated by the beauty of Krishna and his loving companions. These five primary kinds of love that manifest between the soul and God are adoration, service, friendship, parenthood. and romantic love. The spiritual emotions arising from these loving exchanges can only be understood by direct experience."*

Mahaprabhu taught Sanatan for two months and blessed him with divine understanding.

·······

RUPA AND SANATAN EACH PRESERVED what they had learned in writing; whoever studies their books will know the complete path of devotional service to Krishna.

The essence of Sri Chaitanya Mahaprabhu's teaching was somehow to occupy oneself in devotional service to Krishna and thereby develop love for him. He gave Sanatan a dual mission: to educate people by writing books and to uncover the sites of Krishna's pastimes in Vrindavan. In giving him this service, he emphasized to Sanatan that the key to freedom in this world is to see everything and everyone in relation to Krishna.

The Monks of Varanasi

While Mahaprabhu stayed in Varanasi, the people of the town talked about him. They mostly believed in the Advaita philosophy of oneness or nonduality and were followers of the great teacher Shankara, who had lived seven hundred years earlier and whose commentary on Vedanta philosophy had gained wide acceptance all over India. Followers of his teaching believed all beings to be manifestations of God, and the personalities and forms of this world to be part of the great illusion called *maya*. Once the soul rose above this illusion, they taught, its individuality would disappear as it merged into the existence of God, the Source of All. Followers of this philosophy were called Mayavadis.

Spending their time in silent meditation or studying philosophy, the Mayavadi *sannyasis* of Varanasi considered personal devotion to Krishna as intended for beginners on the spiritual path, especially when it involved singing and dancing in public. To them, Mahaprabhu was a sentimentalist, and they openly said so. He didn't complain; instead he avoided their company and bided his time until the opportunity came for him to speak. One of the reasons he had become a *sannyasi* was to meet such people on equal terms, so as to teach them the truth of devotion to Krishna. He waited patiently.

Meanwhile, his small community of devotees living in Varanasi had to hear these criticisms daily. Feeling deeply unhappy, they begged him to do something. If only his critics would meet him personally, his devotees felt, they would experience for themselves his beauty and wisdom, and their hearts would change.

The critics would not have long to wait. A prominent *brahmana* decided to invite all the *sannyasis* of Varanasi to his house for lunch. Receiving acceptances from them all, including Prakashananda Sarasvati, leader of the Mayavadis, this *brahmana* then came personally to invite Mahaprabhu, who agreed to come.

On the appointed day, a large crowd of monks, led by Prakashananda, turned up at the *brahmana*'s house. They found themselves sitting in a big circle, waiting in anticipation for the young *sannyasi* Sri Krishna Chaitanya, about whom they had heard so much. When Mahaprabhu entered the house, all eyes turned to him. Though young, he was broad-shouldered and taller than anyone they had seen; his commanding presence filled the room. When he bowed and offered them a prayer of respect, the *sannyasis* heard his deep voice resonate with authority. In expectant silence, they watched him sit on the bare floor near the door, beside the place for washing feet. Seeing him sit there, as a single body they rose to their feet in wonder and dismay. This effulgent golden personality, whose beautiful face shone like the moon, should not sit there by the door; he should have a seat of honor in their midst.

"Your holiness, please do not sit there," urged Prakashananda as he hurried over to take Mahaprabhu's hand.

"I belong to a lower order of *sannyasis*. I don't deserve to sit with you."

"Nonsense, you must come and sit in the middle," insisted Prakashananda, leading him into the assembly.

Once Mahaprabhu was seated properly, Prakashananda questioned him in front of everyone.

"Sri Krishna Chaitanya, you are a *sannyasi* like us and you belong to our lineage of Shankara, yet you have not come to see us while you have been here in Varanasi. Are you avoiding us? I have another question. A *sannyasi* is supposed to spend his time in meditation and study of Vedanta, so why do you sing and dance in public surrounded by common people and religious sentimentalists? Please explain yourself."

After hearing these questions, Mahaprabhu paused and smiled. Then he spoke with a clear and calm voice.

"My teacher told me I am not qualified to study Vedanta. Instead, he advised me to chant the names of Krishna. He said this chanting would be sufficient to release me from the cycle of birth and death and to bring me to Lord Krishna's lotus feet. He taught me a verse from the scriptures: 'Chant the holy name, chant the holy name, chant the holy name—there is no other way, no other way, no other way to achieve success in this age of Kali.' Since hearing these words, I have not stopped chanting.

"At first, when I chanted I thought I was losing my mind, because I found myself helplessly singing, dancing, laughing, and crying. So I asked my teacher what was happening to me. He told me I was experiencing spiritual ecstasy, the sign of love for God, which is the true result of chanting Hare Krishna. This ecstasy found in Krishna's name is just like an ocean of bliss. Beside this ocean of bliss, your impersonal enlightenment is like a shallow pond. All this my teacher told me.

"He urged me to go on chanting and dancing in the company of devotees without caring what others thought, and to teach this practice of *sankirtan* that will save all people."

Mahaprabhu's words pleased his audience, who could not resist his influence. But they were deeply attached to Vedanta philosophy, which was the foundation of their entire way of life.

"We like what you say and we are happy for you, because you have achieved love for God," said Prakashananda, feeling puzzled. "But why do you avoid studying Vedanta?"

"The verses of the *Vedanta Sutra* were spoken by the Supreme Narayana himself," answered Mahaprabhu, "so they are perfect and without fault. It is not the verses that I avoid, but the interpretations put upon them by Shankara. I mean no disrespect to Shankara, for he is a manifestation of Shiva, but I disagree with his teaching. The Supreme Lord's form is eternal and spiritual, whereas Shankara said it is temporary and made of *maya*.

"We are all eternal sparks of the Supreme Lord, and are forever individuals. The individual souls can never be equal to the original Supreme Soul. We are energy, while God is the source of energy—we are *shakti* and God is *shaktiman*. We are eternal servants, and he is the eternal Lord. On this truth, taught in the Vedanta, Shankara has misled people. Therefore, I say that it is better to hear the original verses of the Vedanta, which all point to Krishna, than to hear the indirect interpretations of Shankara. Whoever hears those interpretations is lost."

Although Mahaprabhu's words contradicted the Mayavadi doctrines, his audience liked them, for he voiced doubts that many of them shared. They wanted to hear more.

"Your holiness, what you say is true," said Prakashananda. "We also are not satisfied with the indirect explanations of our texts. Now please tell us the direct meaning of the *Vedanta Sutra*."

Mahaprabhu replied to Prakashananda: "The Great Spirit described in the Vedanta is the Supreme Person who possesses all qualities and is the source of all truth. By portraying God as impersonal, Shankara denied God's full spiritual nature. The way to know the Supreme Person is to hear about the qualities of God with devotion, under the guidance of a spiritual master. Then you will develop love for God and be freed from material attachment. Such love is the highest goal, for it conquers Krishna and brings the sweet taste of devotional service. Your relationship with God; how to develop that relationship; and love for God; these are the three subjects described in every verse of the *Vedanta Sutra*.

"The author of the *Vedanta Sutra* is Vyasadev. His teacher was Narada Muni, who heard from Brahma, the first created being in the universe, who was taught directly by Vishnu himself. Vyasadev summarized the essential truths of the four *Vedas* and the *Upanishads* in the verses of the *Vedanta Sutras*, then explained their meaning in *Srimad Bhagavatam*, the perfect commentary on the Vedanta and the *Upanishads*. In the *Bhagavatam* he revealed three great truths: the essence of all relationships is Krishna; the essential activity is *bhakti*, devotional service to Krishna; and the ultimate perfection is *prema*, love for Krishna."

Mahaprabhu finished speaking. The effect of his words on all who heard him was to change their hearts forever. From that day on, the *sannayasis* began to chant Krishna's names. No more criticism of Mahaprabhu was heard in Varanasi.

· · ● ● ● ● ● · ·

PEOPLE TALKED ALL OVER TOWN, debating Mahaprabhu's teaching. Many came to visit him and he countered their ideas, logically and with respect. Soon afterward at their ashram, the *sannyasis* gathered to discuss all they had heard. One of their elders voiced his feelings.

"Sri Krishna Chaitanya is right. Renouncing the world without taking up devotional service to Krishna is like beating an empty husk: your labor will be fruitless. Therefore, I say, we should follow his teaching and worship Krishna's divine form, for he is the ultimate Brahman and the cause of everything." Prakashananda heard him and approved.

"The conclusion of Vedanta is that the Ultimate Truth is personal," said Prakashananda. "Although Shankara denied this, his interpretations are misleading. We prefer to accept the words of Sri Krishna Chaitanya, who speaks the truth." After saying this, he started to chant Krishna's names, and led the *sannyasis* out onto the street to chant as well.

There they found Mahaprabhu, who was chanting and dancing in ecstasy with Chandrashekhar, Tapan Mishra, and a crowd of followers. As Prakashananda approached, Mahaprabhu stopped his chanting and bowed to the senior monk. But Prakashananda bowed lower, bending to the ground before him.

"Forgive me Lord," he begged. "Before our meeting, I said many ungenerous things about you. Now by touching your feet I hope to be freed from my offenses, for you are the Supreme Lord Krishna himself."

Mahaprabhu protested, saying he was simply a servant of Krishna. He advised Prakashananda to study *Srimad Bhagavatam* and to always chant the names of the Lord. In this way he would achieve not just liberation, but the ultimate perfection of *prema*, love for God.

During the remainder of Mahaprabhu's stay, Prakashananda and the other *sannyasis* came regularly to see him and to chant with him in public. One day, Mahaprabhu visited the Shiva temple in the heart of Varanasi. A huge crowd gathered and followed him down to the riverside. There, he raised his hands to the sky and everyone spontaneously began to sing, filling the air with the sound of Krishna's names. So it was that the people of Varanasi joined one another in singing the holy names, and the town became like a second Navadvip.

········

IT WAS NEARLY TIME FOR MAHAPRABHU to return to Jagannath Puri. He had been away for almost six months and the hot season was approaching. His devotees living in Varanasi wanted to come with him to Puri, but he asked them to stay behind. Later they could come and visit him, he said; for now he wanted to return as he had come, traveling alone through the forest of Jarikhanda.

Before leaving, he spoke one last time with Sanatan. When they first met in Ramakeli, he had accepted him as his disciple and given him the name Sanatan. Now he made him Sanatan Goswami, recognizing him as one who had mastered his body and mind, and was thus qualified to lead others. Mahaprabhu repeated his earlier wish that Sanatan should go to Vrindavan, where his two brothers had already been sent. There he was to uncover the holy places and write books. Mahaprabhu added to this a special request. In the future, devotees from all over India would be inspired by Mahaprabhu's teachings to come to Vrindavan, either to visit or to stay. Many of them would be poor and destitute, having left everything behind to serve Krishna. He asked Sanatan to organize shelter and spiritual support for all these devotees.

Following this direction, Sanatan Goswami dedicated the remainder of his life to caring for devotees in Vrindavan. His skill and experience in public affairs, coupled with his learning in the scriptures, made him the ideal person to be leader of the Vaishnava community there. Above all these qualities were his deep humility and devotion.

In the following years, Sanatan gave up all comforts and lived in Vrindavan as a mendicant. Wandering among the twelve forests, he shunned permanent shelter, preferring to sleep beneath trees or among the bushes, always remembering Krishna. While he did so he collected the history of the area, revived the holy places associated with Krishna's life, and wrote books about Krishna consciousness.

········

MAHAPRABHU TRAVELED THROUGH THE JARIKHANDA FOREST and reached the outskirts of Jagannath Puri. There he halted while word went ahead to inform the devotees of his arrival. With great excitement they came out to greet him. There were tears and embraces, with much laughter and joy. They brought him to the temple where he saw Jagannath in deep ecstasy, and the priests came out with garlands and offerings from the deities. Finally he was taken to his rooms at Kashi Mishra's house, and a feast was served in his honor by Sarvabhauma Bhattacharya and Svarup Damodar. There his devotees gathered, overflowing onto the street.

Mahaprabhu was only thirty years old, but his outward travels were complete. Now he would stay in Puri in the company of his friends. For the remainder of his life, his journey would lead inward, to the everlasting realm of Radha and Krishna.

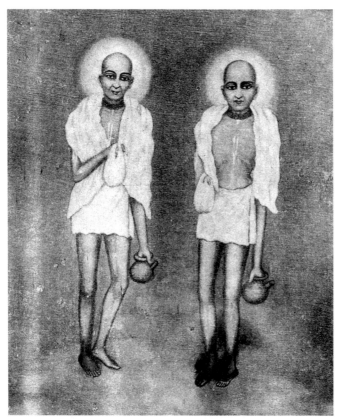

The brothers Rupa and Sanatan were taught directly by Mahaprabhu and preserved his teachings in their writings: Whoever studies their books will know the path of devotion to Krishna.

BOOK FOUR

The Ocean of Love

Rupa and Sanatan in Puri

fter being separated from Mahaprabhu, Rupa Goswami held in his heart the instructions he had received and made them his life's mission. Together with his brother, Anupam, he set off for Vrindavan, contemplating his important task: to write books and thereby share the inspiration and love he had received from Mahaprabhu. Upon reaching Vrindavan, the brothers toured the twelve forests as their master had. All the while Rupa sought inspiration for his writing, wondering where he would begin. He decided to compose a drama about the love between Krishna and his companions in Vrindavan.

In his drama, Rupa would show Krishna's love for Radha in the forest, as well as his love for Queen Satyabhama in Dvaraka city. In the forest, Krishna lived as a cowherd boy, whereas in Dvaraka he lived as a king. These two lives showed different sides of Krishna and the love between his companions: the intimate love in the forest of Vrindavan, and the reverential love in the royal city of Dvaraka. He started to compose some verses, but without the company of his elder brother he was uncertain how to proceed. He longed to see Mahaprabhu again, to seek guidance and encouragement.

From Vrindavan, Rupa and Anupam returned to Varanasi, hoping to find Mahaprabhu still there, but by the time they arrived he had already left for Puri. They also discovered that Sanatan had recently left Varanasi for

Vrindavan by a different route, passing his brothers on the way without their knowledge. Rupa and Anupam stayed in Varanasi for a few days, as guests of Mahaprabhu's devotees, hearing all about his meetings with Sanatan and his success with the Mayavadi *sannyasis*, then continued on their way to Puri. Their route was through Bengal, where they visited their family in Ramakeli.

On the journey, Anupam suddenly fell ill and passed away by the banks of the Ganges.

Rupa was bereft of his brother's company, and his thoughts dwelt even more on Mahaprabhu and the service he had been given. He pressed on alone to Jagannath Puri, thinking deeply about how best to structure his drama. One night he had a stirring dream. A goddess appeared to him and blessed him saying, "Write a drama just about me, and I promise you it will be wonderful." On waking, Rupa understood that he had received divine inspiration from Satyabhama, Krishna's queen in Dvaraka. Her wishes seemed clear: whereas he had planned to write one drama, she wanted him to write two separate works, one about Krishna, the cowherd boy in Vrindavan, and one about Krishna, the royal prince in Dvaraka. Queen Satyabhama's spirited personality, as told in the sacred *Bhagavatam*, would make her a good subject for Rupa's tale of Dvaraka, complementing the story he would tell of Radha's love for Krishna in Vrindavan. Yet Rupa remained undecided.

When he arrived in Puri, Rupa found the town full of Mahaprabhu's devotees from Bengal, there to celebrate the Rathayatra festival.

Puri was a seat of Hindu orthodoxy, and in this setting Rupa was conscious of his Muslim background. He was born a high-caste Hindu, but he had been recruited into government service and so had lived and worked most of his life among Muslims as if he were one of them, contrary to strict brahminical practice. When he had first met Mahaprabhu in Ramakeli, he had made friends with Haridas Thakur; the two of them found they shared a connection with Islam, for Haridas had been raised a Muslim. Rupa therefore went to find Haridas in his humble cottage beside the seashore, the one given to him by Mahaprabhu. Here the elderly Haridas spent his time absorbed in chanting Krishna's names. He gladly welcomed the cultured young Vaishnava into his small shelter and gave him a place to stay, promising Rupa he would soon meet Mahaprabhu.

It was Mahaprabhu's custom each day to visit Haridas. His routine was to see Jagannath's lunchtime offering at the temple, then bathe in the sea and recite his noon mantras. On his way to the beach he would bring Haridas *prasadam* from the temple, and pause to speak with him for a while. At noon on the very day of Rupa's arrival, Mahaprabhu appeared at Haridas's cottage as usual.

"Rupa Goswami has come to see you, my Lord," informed Haridas, as Rupa prostrated himself in the sand.

Sri Krishna Chaitanya was pleased to see his young disciple again, and spoke with him for a while. Rupa told him of the untimely death of his brother Anupam. Mahaprabhu asked after Sanatan, and heard how the brothers had missed each other on the road.

The following day, Mahaprabhu introduced Rupa to all the devotees, and asked Advaita Acharya and Nityananda to give him their blessings so that he could write about *bhakti-rasa*, the emotions of divine love. The Vaishnavas welcomed Rupa and accepted him as their brother.

While in Puri, Rupa continued to write his poetry about the loving affairs of Krishna and his devotees. One day, while Mahaprabhu was with Haridas, he happened to say something to Rupa.

"Krishna never leaves Vrindavan. When he is away from Vrindavan he becomes Vasudev Krishna, an expansion of the original Krishna."

Rupa thought deeply over these words. Ever since he had heard from Satyabhama in his dream that in his writings he should keep Krishna in Vrindavan apart from Krishna in Dvaraka, he had been meditating on how best to distinguish the pastoral atmosphere of Vrindavan from the grander atmosphere of Dvaraka. Now he decided he must divide his drama into two distinct works.

Rupa longed to receive further guidance from Mahaprabhu about his writing. He wanted to know if his compositions would be pleasing to him. His opportunity came in an unexpected way, when he witnessed for the first time Mahaprabhu's dance of ecstasy at Rathayatra. Rupa heard him sing the words of Radha—words that only Svarup understood. When Rupa heard Mahaprabhu's song he instinctively realized the whole context of his master's words—why he sang as Radha and what memories he was evoking.

Hurrying to his cottage absorbed in these thoughts, Rupa composed a Sanskrit verse to express Radha's conflicting feelings of love for Krishna.

"Hear me, dear friend," he wrote in the voice of Radha addressing a friend. "Now I have met my lover of old, Krishna, on the field of Kurukshetra. I am the same Radha and he is the same Krishna. We are meeting in happiness as before. But still I long to be with him beneath the trees on the bank of the

Yamuna, where I can hear his flute playing the sweet fifth note in the forest of Vrindavan."

He inscribed this verse on a palm leaf and hid it in the thatched roof inside his cottage before leaving to bathe in the sea. While he was gone, Mahaprabhu arrived with Svarup and saw the palm leaf. Taking it down and reading it, he was surprised by Rupa's words, so he sat and waited for him.

"Dear Rupa, how could you know what was in my heart?" he said when Rupa returned, to which Rupa bowed in silent reverence.

"You must have blessed him with your special mercy," said Svarup, "for your inner thoughts are a secret no one can guess."

"Rupa came to me in Prayag," replied Mahaprabhu, "and I revealed many secrets to him there. Now, while he is here with us in Puri, I want you to teach him all you know about *bhakti-rasa*."

Svarup gladly accepted this request, and over the coming months he educated Rupa in the secrets of the loving affairs of Radha and Krishna. Rupa stayed on in Puri after the Bengali devotees had all returned to their homes. He received more and more encouragement and inspiration, and made good progress in writing his two dramas.

One day, Mahaprabhu came to see Rupa and Haridas. Seeing several leaves of Rupa's manuscript, he held them up with admiration.

"Rupa's handwriting is like a row of pearls," he declared. "Let me see what he has written." As he read through the manuscript, one particular Sanskrit verse caught his attention. He chanted it aloud.

"I do not know how much nectar these two syllables *krish-na* have produced. When the holy name of Krishna is chanted, it appears to dance within my mouth. I then desire many, many mouths. When that name enters my ears, I desire many millions of ears. When the holy name dances in the courtyard of my heart, it conquers my mind, and my senses become inert."

Haridas, whose sole occupation was to chant Krishna's names day and night, danced for joy when he heard this verse. Mahaprabhu wanted his close friends to hear the beauty of Rupa's poetry, so the following day he brought Sarvabhauma and Ramananda to the cottage.

Mahaprabhu sat them down and asked Rupa to chant the verse that had so impressed him. Rupa was too modest to speak, so Svarup sang it for him. When the others heard the verse, about Radha's longing for Vrindavan, they understood, as Svarup had before them, that such insights into Mahaprabhu's mind were possible only for someone who had received his special favor.

Rupa was eventually persuaded to chant his verse in glorification of Krishna's name. Upon hearing it, everyone was full of praise.

Ramananda, who was considered by all to be the expert on *rasa*, wanted to question Rupa. What was he writing, and could he recite more of his poetry? Rupa was hesitant, but verse by verse he revealed his poetic jewels. The more he revealed, the more they were stunned. Their respect and love grew for this gentle Vaishnava, whose words spoke so profoundly and sweetly of the deep emotions of the soul. For a long time, the company sat together, appreciating the different moods of love for Krishna. They heard verses from the opening scenes of the two dramas Rupa was composing— first describing Vrindavan, then Krishna, then Radharani and her innermost thoughts. Rupa was uplifted by their loving appreciation, yet humbled by the attention paid to him.

"In your presence I feel overwhelmed, like a glow worm in the sunshine," he said. But still Ramananda urged him on. Rupa made the Sanskrit language sing as he evoked the subtle shades of spiritual love, just as Mahaprabhu had known he would, and all present gave him their affectionate blessings.

Rupa stayed with Haridas for a few days more, and then it was time to leave. He had been in Puri for ten months, during which time he felt he had been profoundly enriched by being accepted into Mahaprabhu's inner circle.

"Now go and stay in Vrindavan," Mahaprabhu bade him. "Write wonderful books and help Sanatan uncover Krishna's holy places. Together, the two of you will teach everyone about devotional service to Krishna. One day, I will come and visit you there. Until then, serve me in that holy place." Then he added, "Tell Sanatan that he also should come here and visit me."

Mahaprabhu embraced him and Rupa Goswami, weeping, placed his head at his master's feet. With farewells ringing in his ears he left, traveling first to Bengal and then on to Vrindavan.

In the years that followed, having heard the secrets of devotion from Chaitanya Mahaprabhu, and being blessed by his devotees to realize these truths in his heart, Rupa Goswami wrote many books. His two dramas about Krishna, named *Vidagdha-Madhava* and *Lalita-Madhava*, were eventually completed. His greatest work was called *Bhakti Rasamrita Sindhu* ("The Ocean of the Nectar of Devotion"), the definitive treatise on the complete art of *bhakti-rasa*, the emotions of divine love. Its opening words are "Insignificant though I am, I pray to the lotus feet of Mahaprabhu, the Supreme Lord in my heart. He inspired me to write this book."

········

EVEN AS RUPA MADE HIS WAY BACK TO BENGAL and Vrindavan, his brother Sanatan was traversing the great Jarikhanda Forest of central India. Like Rupa, he had stayed for some time in Vrindavan before deciding to visit Mahaprabhu in Jagannath Puri. He wanted to avoid being seen in Bengal, so he followed the same cross-country route taken by Mahaprabhu earlier that year. By the time he reached Puri he was weak from fasting, and suffering from a skin infection caused by contaminated water in the forest. He felt acutely uncomfortable as he approached Puri, his body covered in infectious sores. He considered himself an outcast among Hindus because of his former involvement with the Muslim rulers.

"What is the use of this wretched body?" he thought despairingly. "No one wants me here and I will not even be able to see Mahaprabhu, who lives among the high-caste priests close to the temple." Filled with these gloomy thoughts he resolved to put an end to his life by throwing himself beneath the wheels of Jagannatha's chariot in the presence of his master.

As Rupa had done before him, Sanatan looked for Haridas Thakur as the one he knew and trusted to understand his feelings. Haridas welcomed him to his cottage, embracing him as a dear friend. That day, when Mahaprabhu came on his daily visit to Haridas, he was surprised to discover Sanatan. He opened his arms to embrace his beloved devotee, but Sanatan backed away.

"Don't touch me, Lord, I beg you. I am an outcast and my body is covered with sores. Just let me lie in the dust at your feet." Despite these words, Mahaprabhu held Sanatan tightly in his arms and then introduced him to his companions.

Sanatan stayed with Haridas. Time passed, while together they chanted Krishna's names. In the distance, they could see the pinnacle of Jagannath's temple; this was the nearest either of them permitted themselves to come to the temple, where the strict rules of the caste *brahmanas* forbade temple access to non-Hindus. But each day, Mahaprabhu came to see them, bringing *prasadam* from the temple and staying to talk about Krishna.

One day, to Sanatan's surprise, Mahaprabhu brought up the topic of suicide.

"It is true that a devotee who loves Krishna finds it hard to be apart from him in this world, and so sometimes desires death. But to deliberately take your own life will never bring you closer to Krishna. The only way to reach Krishna is through loving service. Don't think your body is unfit for serving Krishna, for even the most insignificant person is qualified for his service. Merely by serving Krishna you become exalted, whereas the

Mahaprabhu gazed into Jagannath's eyes as he danced in front of his chariot. He appeared like a spinning circle of fire. Crying out the names of Krishna, he leaped high into the air, tears streaming from his eyes (see page 103).

The King came disguised as an ordinary devotee and found Mahaprabhu asleep in the garden. He sat at his feet and sang softly of the gopis' love for Krishna. Hearing his poetry Mahaprabhu awoke and embraced him (see page 105).

For ten days Mahaprabhu taught Rupa about Krishna, about service to Krishna, and about the intricate secrets of loving relationships between Krishna and his devotees (see page 119).

Sanatan arrived at the house where Mahaprabhu was staying. Appearing like an unshaven Muslim mendicant, he sat patiently outside the door. Mahaprabhu knew he was there and asked for him to be called inside (see page 121).

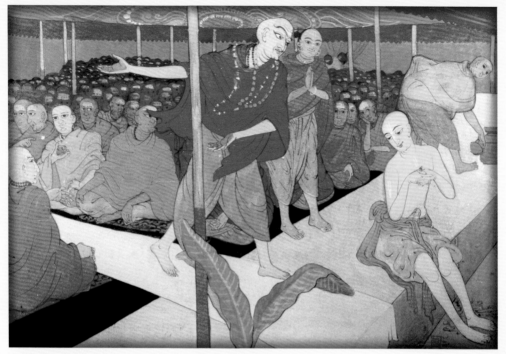

*A large crowd of monks sat in a big circle, waiting for the young sannyasi to arrive.
When Mahaprabhu came, he sat on the bare floor near the door. Prakashananda hurried
over and lead him to the centre of the room (see page 126).*

*Prakashananda and the sannyasis saw Mahaprabhu chanting and dancing in ecstasy with
his followers. In front of everyone Prakashananda bowed to the ground before him, begging
his forgiveness (see page 129).*

Placing Sanatan under the watchful care of the elderly Haridas, Mahaprabhu embraced them both, then left for the beach (see page 141).

Mahaprabhu stood at the back of the Jagannath temple beside the Garuda column. There he would enter a trance, seeing only the form of Krishna playing his flute in Vrindavan (see page 150).

Haridas held Mahaprabhu's feet to his chest and fixed his eyes upon his shining face. While chanting Krishna's names, tears coursing down his cheeks, he gave up his life in front of everyone (see page 153).

Mahaprabhu raised Haridas's body and danced with it down to the sea. There they bathed the body and interred it in a grave near the shore, dug in the sand with their bare hands (see page 154).

On a full moon night Mahaprabhu walked with his friends along the seashore, lost in thoughts of Krishna.
Suddenly, unseen by anyone, he ran headlong into the waves (see page 157).

Previous pages: When Chaitanya chanted and danced, he created waves of spiritual ecstacy.

greatest personalities in this world, if they do not serve Krishna, are of no consequence. There are many ways to serve Krishna, of which the best is to chant his name in all humility, for that brings you the gift of pure love. Give up your morbid thoughts, Sanatan, and chant Krishna's name. Then you will achieve his shelter." Hearing these words, Sanatan fell at his master's feet.

"You knew all that was in my mind, Lord. I am indeed the lowest—what use can I be to you?"

"Your body belongs to me and through you I have important work to do," Mahaprabhu assured him. "You will teach about many things: how to be a devotee; how to love Krishna; and the character and behavior of Vaishnavas. You will establish pilgrimage places in Krishna's sacred homeland of Mathura and Vrindavan."

Sanatan was astonished to hear these words. In wonder he prayed: "Master, make me your instrument. Make me dance like a puppet who dances without knowing what he is doing."

Placing Sanatan under Haridas's watchful care, Mahaprabhu embraced them both and left. Watching him leave, Haridas congratulated Sanatan.

"Your good fortune cannot be measured, for all these things will certainly come to pass. You will do wonderful service. As for me, I am of no use."

"Haridas, no one chants Krishna's name with more faith and devotion than you," replied Sanatan with conviction. "Each day you chant 300,000 holy names. Through you, Mahaprabhu is teaching everyone. Some live good lives but do not teach; others teach but do not live good lives. You, however, do both. You are ideal in every way."

········

THE SUMMER HEAT ARRIVED. Along the seashore the sands burned under the blazing sun. One day, Mahaprabhu sent word for Sanatan to join him for lunch in a favorite seaside garden. Not wanting to pass in front of the temple gate, Sanatan walked along the beach. He was so intent on seeing Mahaprabhu that he did not notice the hot sand. By the time he reached the garden, his feet were blistered and burned. Mahaprabhu was dismayed. He nonetheless understood Sanatan's motive in avoiding the path past the temple entrance so that his presence would not disturb the orthodox priests going about their service, and he thanked him.

"Sanatan, only you have the humility to behave like this. I am pleased with you for respecting the temple customs. Good behavior is the ornament of a devotee." Once again, although Sanatan was reluctant to allow his master to touch his diseased body, Mahaprabhu embraced him. On this and other occasions, Sanatan felt blessed, but still he was unhappy. He confided in Haridas that he could not stay in Puri because he was causing offense by letting Mahaprabhu embrace him. News of his continued anxiety reached Mahaprabhu's ears.

"My dear Sanatan, I hold you in deep regard and affection—please do not leave. You are deeply learned in the scriptures, with the power to teach even me. I love you just like my own child. The sores on your body don't offend me any more than a baby offends its mother. As a mother, I find you faultless; I see your body as all-spiritual. Now let me bless you again." So saying, he embraced Sanatan yet again. As he did so, Sanatan's sores vanished and his skin glowed golden. From that day he was cured.

Summer passed, Sanatan lamented no more, and the time for Rathayatra came. Sanatan met the devotees from Bengal, and they befriended him as they had Rupa. The time came for him to return to Vrindavan. His parting with Mahaprabhu held joy mixed with sadness, for they would not meet again.

Sanatan Goswami retraced his footsteps through the Jarikhanda Forest. He stopped at all the places where Mahaprabhu had halted, and heard about him from the local inhabitants. At last, a year after his departure, he returned to Vrindavan. Rupa Goswami, after settling their affairs in Bengal and dividing their remaining wealth among their relatives and the *brahmanas*, joined his brother in Vrindavan. For the rest of their lives, the two brothers worked to serve their master's orders. They gathered scriptures and used their evidence to unearth the lost holy places associated with the life of Krishna. They established beautiful temples of Krishna, particularly the temple dedicated to Madan Mohan founded by Sanatan, and the temple dedicated to Govinda founded by Rupa. For themselves, they wished for no comforts. They lived simply, depending on the charity of householders as they moved from one grove to another without permanent shelter. Preferring to sleep beneath the stars, sheltered by the sacred trees of Vrindavan, they spent their time serving Krishna's devotees, writing books, and chanting Krishna's names.

Sanatan Goswami's most important book was the *Brihad Bhagavatamrita*, which focused on the following themes: the nature of a devotee; how to perform devotional service; and the truth about Krishna. He also wrote the

Hari Bhakti Vilasa, to teach how to live in this world as a devotee, and other books. His writings became the foundation for the Krishna consciousness movement in years to come.

Haridas, Teacher of the Name

Every day in Jagannath Puri, Mahaprabhu visited Haridas Thakur and talked with him about Krishna. Haridas constantly chanted the names of Krishna, so Mahaprabhu's followers called him Namacharya, "teacher of the name".

One day, Mahaprabhu thought about all the people suffering in this world of birth and death.

"Dear Haridas, how will the souls of this age ever be freed?" he asked.

"They can all be freed by chanting the holy name," assured Haridas. "Take the example of Ajamil, as described in the *Srimad Bhagavatam*. He named his youngest son Narayan, a name for God. When he was an old man, in distress he called his son's name, without thinking that in so doing he was calling on the name of God. As a result he was liberated. When people pronounce the syllables of God's name, such as *ra-ma*, even unintentionally in the course of casual conversation, they are purified. Since they are not consciously calling on the name of God, their chanting is without offense. The holy name is so powerful that even such a shadow of the holy name will free the soul from material life." Mahaprabhu was consoled by Haridas's words, but still he wanted to know more.

"What of the animals, trees, and insects who are incapable of chanting—how will they be freed?" he asked.

"They too will be saved," replied Haridas. "You have chanted the holy name loudly, and your followers are also chanting. As the name echoes around the world all living beings are purified. The echo that we hear is the chanting of all creation, reverberating with the sacred sound. You have set in motion the liberation of the entire universe. As old souls are liberated, new souls come to take their place, and they also hear the holy name. So there is no end to your mercy."

All his life Haridas had embraced this simple and profound teaching of the all-powerful mercy of Krishna's holy name. As a young man he had experienced it for himself. He was raised in a Muslim community in East

Bengal, but was orphaned at an early age. When he first found faith in Krishna he thought himself unqualified, because of his Muslim upbringing, to worship in temples and public places. So he put his full faith in Krishna's name and started to chant continuously. He vowed that each day he would chant 300,000 names, even though this took him all day and night, leaving only an hour or two for sleeping and eating.

Haridas saw all around him that people were suffering. While Advaita prayed in Shantipur, Haridas chanted fervently, praying for the Lord to descend into this world and teach people the path of pure love for God. People thought Haridas a saint and began to worship him. But the local magistrate was envious of his popularity. Seeing that Haridas was young and handsome, he paid a beautiful prostitute to tempt him to break his vows.

When Haridas was alone at night, the girl came to his cottage in the forest and offered herself to him. But he would not be distracted from chanting, and as long as he continued chanting, her charms were rendered powerless. For three nights, she stayed beside him, waiting for him to satisfy her. But as each night passed, the sun rose with not a pause in the flow of his chanting. The beautiful girl sat there listening to the soothing sound of Krishna's name chanted from the lips of a pure soul. Gradually, her will evaporated along with the shadows of the night. At sunrise, after the third night, she fell at his feet begging his mercy and forgiveness. Haridas, who had stayed only for her benefit, initiated her with the Hare Krishna mantra, gave her his seat and hermit's dwelling, and left that place never to return. She stayed and chanted Krishna's name as his faithful disciple for the rest of her life. In time, many people came to learn from her and also found faith in the power of Krishna's names.

People had never seen such steadfastness and faith in Krishna's names as possessed by Haridas. From village to village, his fame spread and he attracted the attention of the Muslim rulers, who feared his influence among the people. The local ruler had him imprisoned and beaten so severely that he was taken for dead. But Haridas never stopped chanting, and he miraculously survived and escaped.

He reached the village of Chandapur near the Ganges, where he was sheltered by Vaishnavas in a hermit's cottage. Here he was visited daily by a young boy, whom he taught and blessed with attachment for Krishna's holy names. This boy later surrendered himself to Mahaprabhu as Raghunath Das Goswami.

One day, a meeting was held by the local *brahmanas,* and Haridas was invited to speak about the power of the holy name. The Vaishnavas used to meet and chant together, but other people mocked their faith in Vishnu. So they called upon Haridas to speak in favor of chanting.

"As the rising sun drives away the ocean of darkness from this world, so chanting the name of God even once banishes all the effects of a person's sinful life," declared Haridas. Then he further explained: "When the first light of dawn touches the horizon, even before sunrise, ghosts flee; then when the sun appears in fullness, the day begins. In the same way, the holy name, though imperfectly chanted, brings liberation; then when the name is chanted with faith and reverence, it awakens the soul's pure love for Krishna. This love is worth infinitely more than liberation."

Haridas's teaching on the holy name was greatly appreciated by his audience. But one *brahmana* was unconvinced.

"Why must you chant so loud? Isn't it better to contemplate silently?"

"By chanting silently you benefit your own soul," replied Haridas, "But by chanting aloud you purify all who hear, even those in the form of plants and animals who cannot chant for themselves."

Eventually, Haridas came to Shantipur, where Advaita Acharya gave him shelter in a cave by the Ganges. Here, Haridas continued his incessant chanting undisturbed. Advaita was the leader of the *brahmanas*, and he publicly glorified Haridas at their annual ceremony to honor departed souls. After this, no one dared criticize him for his faith in Krishna's name. He and Advaita became close companions and spent long hours immersed in talking about Krishna.

Nearby in Navadvip, the young Nimai Pandit, the one whose appearance they had both prayed for, foresook his life as a teacher of grammar and started his *sankirtan* movement. Haridas was among the first to join him, going out with Nityananda to preach from door to door. He led one of the three groups of chanters who encircled the Kazi's house. When Mahaprabhu became a *sannyasi* and moved to Jagannath Puri, Haridas followed him there. By this time, Haridas was in middle age, and Mahaprabhu respected him as his teacher and mentor. The fact that Haridas did not belong to the *brahmana* caste, and was born a Muslim, gave him special significance. He demonstrated the universality of Mahaprabhu's teaching. So long as he was faithfully chanting he was a living example of devotion to Krishna's name, giving hope to all people. This was why Mahaprabhu used to see Haridas daily.

Sharing Love for God

The devotees of Bengal couldn't live without Mahaprabhu. During his youth, he was their life and soul, and when he left them and moved to Puri they never got over the loss. Each year they went on pilgrimage to see him in Puri, where they stayed from the time of Rathayatra in June until the end of September.

Traveling was risky, for there were bandits in some parts and the borders between the warring kingdoms of Bengal and Orissa were well guarded. There were taxes and tolls to pay, and rivers and estuaries to navigate through the coastal lands of the Bay of Bengal. Guiding a group of two hundred or more pilgrims over the distance of three hundred miles needed careful organization. This responsibility fell to a physician named Shivananda Sen, who knew the roads well. He collected financial contributions, arranged meals and lodgings, and paid tolls and boat charges.

Each year, the group carried gifts for Mahaprabhu, among which were three large bags of sweets and savories. This custom was started by Raghava Pandit and his sister, Damayanti, who lived in Panihati. They were expert cooks who had many times entertained Mahaprabhu in their home, where they enjoyed a special relationship with him based on their lavishly cooked offerings. Mahaprabhu kept the bags with him all year, tasting something new each day and sharing it with his guests in Puri. This reminded him of the love of his devotees in Navadvip.

One year, Shivananda adopted a stray dog as one of the party. The Vaishnavas welcomed the dog as a fellow soul, a servant of Krishna. Shivananda paid the ferrymen along the way to take the dog on their boats with the rest of them. One evening, he was detained and no one remembered to feed the animal. As a consequence, as day broke the next morning, the dog was missing. They spent a long time searching, but in the end they had to continue without their faithful follower.

The party arrived in Puri just as Mahaprabhu and his friends were setting off for the lake called Narendra Sarovara, where an annual water festival was held. They sang and danced their way to the lakeside, where they plunged into the water with Mahaprabhu in their midst, all playfully splashing about. Time seemed to stand still. They felt as if they had entered the eternal pastimes of Vrindavan, in which the cowherd boys played with Krishna in the Yamuna.

Floating in an ocean of ecstasy, calling the names of Krishna and Chaitanya, they laughed and called out with joy, while on the shore others danced and sang the holy names.

After playing in the water, they got dressed and followed Mahaprabhu to the great temple to see Jagannath. Each time Mahaprabhu saw Jagannath, it was as if he saw him for the first time. He would gaze at the deity's enormous black eyes and entrancing smile, and was unable to stop his tears. When the devotees saw this, their hearts melted and they would also weep. They saw before them their two Lords together: the one who stood in the temple and the one who moved among them sharing his love for Krishna. It was as if Jagannath, attracted by the sound of their chanting, had come in person to chant with them.

The next morning, the pilgrims from Bengal visited Mahaprabhu in his room and were amazed to find their friend, the missing dog, sitting on the terrace happily chewing coconut pulp fed to him by Mahaprabhu from his own plate.

"This animal has the highest good fortune," they exclaimed. "Eating the remnants of Sri Chaitanya's plate bestows love for God." They were astonished, however, at what happened next.

"Chant the holy name of Krishna!" laughed Mahaprabhu to the dog.

"Krishna! Krishna!" cried the dog, while chewing on the coconut pulp.

Shivananda bowed his head to the ground before the dog, begging forgiveness for his neglect. Over the next four days, the dog again could not be found, and they guessed the fortunate creature had left this world, liberated by the mercy of Mahaprabhu.

Whenever the devotees arrived from Bengal, there would be a huge *kirtan*. Sometimes Mahaprabhu divided them into seven groups, each with a principal dancer, such as Nityananda or Advaita. Then he mystically entered each group, to appear in seven places at once. Crowds of onlookers, including the King and his queens, watched from a distance, and the sound of the chanting pierced the air like shimmering thunder, causing people's hair to stand on end. Drums beat and cymbals clashed, as the devotees swam in the nectar of Krishna's name.

"My head falls at the feet of Jagannath," sang Mahaprabhu over and over again.

Sometimes he fell unconscious on the ground, and then rising again his body trembled like a leaf in the wind. No one noticed the passing of time as the chanters drank in Mahaprabhu's love, until Nityananda became aware that it was late afternoon and everyone was exhausted. He called a halt and they went with Mahaprabhu to bathe in the ocean, after which they ate together on the beach.

········

ONCE THE VISITING DEVOTEES were settled in their various accommodations, as arranged by Shivananda Sen, they came one by one to meet Mahaprabhu. Some were his friends since childhood. For example, there was the sweet-maker, Parameshvara. When Mahaprabhu was a little boy, he used to visit Parameshvara's house and was given sweets every time he came. Now the elderly man came to visit him.

"Parameshvara, how good it is to see you after all these years," said Mahaprabhu, asking after his family. These simple exchanges filled the devotees with happiness. Just to see Mahaprabhu and be ackowledged by him was their greatest satisfaction.

"You all go through so much difficulty to come here, leaving behind your homes and families to take a dangerous journey. I should stop you, but then I would miss you too much. I am a mendicant with no money. How can I repay you for coming to see me year after year? I have only this body, which I give to you. Do with me as you wish."

········

WHILE THEY STAYED IN PURI, the devotees took turns inviting Mahaprabhu to lunch. Staying in their different quarters, they cooked for him. One year, when Advaita Acharya's turn came, he and his wife, Sita, cooked Mahaprabhu's favorite preparations. When Advaita cooked, he became fully absorbed in his work. On this occasion, however, he was distracted by the thought that Mahaprabhu would not come alone: he would be arriving with a crowd of *sannyasis*; Advaita and Sita would not have the happiness of receiving him as their only guest.

While he was immersed in his cooking, and entertaining these slight reservations, a tropical storm arose. The sky turned dark, lightning flashed, and thunder rolled. Then a deluge of hail followed by torrential rain swept through the landscape on high winds. The *sannyasis*, who were about to set out to meet Mahaprabhu at Advaita's house, abandoned their lunch appointment and stayed in their residences. Advaita, expecting no one would come, called Mahaprabhu in meditation to come and eat, and while reciting prayers mentally offered him the completed dishes.

"Hare Krishna," heard Advaita. He looked around and to his surprise, saw Mahaprabhu enter the room, untouched by the rain. Overcome with joy, Advaita gave his master a seat and washed his feet, according to custom. Then he and Sita served him each preparation until he had eaten everything they had cooked.

"No one cooks as sweetly as you do," said Mahaprabhu. Advaita and Sita beamed with happiness. Their desires were fulfilled.

"Dear Lord, please never leave us," they prayed. "Let us serve you eternally."

········

EACH YEAR, WHEN IT WAS TIME for the devotees to return to Bengal, the parting became more difficult. One year, Mahaprabhu spoke earnestly with Nityananda.

"I have in the past asked you to remain in Bengal all year round, but still you come here to see me. I know you come out of love, but I have a special request. Please do not come again—stay in Bengal. I will be there with you."

Thereafter, Nityananda stayed in Bengal and served Mahaprabhu as he had asked. He spoke of his master always, and when people saw him, brightly dressed amid his exuberant followers and filled with infectious joy of love for God, their hearts filled with joy and they, too, became followers of Mahaprabhu.

There were some in Bengal, however, who did not appreciate Nityananda's uninhibited ways. Among them was a *brahmana* of Navadvip who in his youth had been a student of Mahaprabhu and was now his faithful devotee. When he saw Nityananda's method of presentation, he was doubtful. "How could such a flamboyant and unconventional person as Nityananda represent Mahaprabhu?" he thought. This doubt preyed on his mind, so he left for Jagannath Puri, where he visited Mahaprabhu every day and sat at his feet, until one day, when he found they were alone, he took the chance to express his doubt.

"Nityananda wanders around Navadvip wearing golden ornaments and brightly colored silks, and I cannot understand him. He chews intoxicating betel nuts and disregards all conventions. People say he is a *sannyasi* and a great soul. Why then does he not behave as a *sannyasi* should? My heart is full of doubt. If you think I can understand, please tell me the truth about him."

Mahaprabhu saw the question was a sincere one, so he carefully answered him.

"I regard Nityananda as untouched by fault, as a lotus leaf is untouched by water. Krishna says in the *Srimad Bhagavatam*, 'My pure devotees have neither faults nor virtues because they have attained me, who am above all material concepts.' As Krishna is beyond good or bad, so is his pure devotee.

"Furthermore, Krishna says, 'If you find fault with my devotee, even though you worship me and chant my name, you will find many obstacles in your path. On the other hand, if you love my devotee, you will certainly attain me.'

"Instead of dwelling on the faults that you see, please try to love the person regardless of faults or virtues. For example, suppose you were to see Nityananda in a wineshop with a girl on his arm, still you are to love him. If you love him, you love me. This is the truth."

When he heard these words, the *brahmana* found that his doubts had left him and faith in Nityananda arose in his heart. He returned peacefully to Navadvip, where he joined with Nityananda, who accepted him, as he accepted all who sought his help.

The Care of Friends

After another six years, when Mahaprabhu was thirty-six years old, the visits from Bengal ceased, and he withdrew to his close circle of friends. Still, he visited Jagannath. From the time Mahaprabhu first arrived in Puri, he had visited the temple every day to see the deity of Jagannath. Remembering what had happened on that first occasion, when he had upset the temple attendants by falling unconscious on the floor in front of the deity, he stayed at the back of the temple so as not to disturb anyone. He used to stand beside the Garuda column, which held Garuda, the bird-carrier of Vishnu, kneeling with folded hands ready to serve his master in the form of Jagannath.

By this column was where Mahaprabhu would always be found when he was in the temple. Sometimes, while in this spot, he would enter a trance in which he was unaware of his surroundings, gazing at Jagannath and seeing only the form of Krishna playing his flute in Vrindavan. Floods of tears would fall from his lotus eyes and collect in a depression at the foot of the column. When eventually he withdrew his gaze, his ecstasy would subside.

"Where has Krishna gone?" he would despairingly ask of those nearby. "Where is Vrindavan? Where is that beautiful cowherd who plays the flute?"

At times such as these, when Mahaprabhu was in apparent distress due to his intense emotions, he lost all sense of time and place, and needed to be cared for by his friends. These fortunate ones who gathered close supported him as he became more and more absorbed in love for Krishna.

His faithful servant Govinda many times protected him when he was in this oblivious state. Govinda never left his side and tended to his every need. Once, after a long, ecstatic *kirtan*, Mahaprabhu was so tired from dancing that when he reached the doorway to his room, he dropped to the floor and fell into a deep sleep. Govinda came to massage his legs, as he usually did after a *kirtan*, but found he could not enter the room because his master was lying in the doorway. He asked him to move so he could go in to massage his feet.

"I am too tired to move," murmured Mahaprabhu.

"But unless you move I cannot massage your feet," said Govinda.

"Do as you wish—I am unable to move."

Govinda thought it would be disrespectful for him to step over his master's body, but if he did not, he could not serve him. So he carefully stepped over him and then sat down to massage his feet. When he had finished, instead of leaving to eat his lunch, he sat and waited. After some time, Mahaprabhu awoke.

"You are still here? Why did you not go to eat?"

"I could not leave because you are blocking the door."

"You could have left by the same way you came in."

Govinda said nothing, but thought to himself, "I will commit a hundred offenses to serve you, my Lord, but none to serve myself."

·•••••••·

JAGADANANDA WAS A COMPANION OF MAHAPRABHU, whose relationship with him was sometimes stormy because of his intense loving attachment. He had been with him since the early days in Navadvip, and followed him to Puri.

Once, Jagadananda brought a large pitcher of sandalwood oil as a gift, which he had transported with great effort from Navadvip. He gave it to Govinda and asked him to use a little every day for Mahaprabhu's massage. But the oil was perfumed, and Mahaprabhu was unwilling to use it.

"When people smell this perfume on my body, they will think me one of those false *sannyasis* who keeps women," he told Govinda. "Give it to the temple to be burned in the lamps on Jagannath's altar, then Jagadananda's labors will be put to good use."

When Jagadananda heard from Govinda that his gift had been refused, he was hurt. He came to see Mahaprabhu, and was about to speak when Mahaprabhu spoke first: "I appreciate your gift, Jagadananda, bringing this oil all the way from Bengal, but I am a *sannyasi* and I cannot accept it. Please give it to the temple for the service of Jagannath's lamps. That will be a good use for it."

"Who told you this? I never brought any oil from Bengal," Jagadananda replied with tears in his eyes. Then he heaved the clay jug into the courtyard and dashed it to the ground, smashing it into a thousand pieces. After this, he locked himself in his room, where he fasted and refused all entreaties to come out.

After three days, Mahaprabhu came and spoke to him.

"Jagadananda!" he called through the door. "I want you to cook for me today. I am going to the temple now and I will be back at noon."

Jagadananda got up and bathed. He felt better now. By the time Mahaprabhu returned, he had cooked a feast with the help of his friends. He washed Mahaprabhu's feet and placed a banana leaf plate before him, piled high with many kinds of vegetable preparations.

"I will not eat alone, Jagadananda. Make another plate for yourself and join me."

"I will eat as soon as I have served you," replied Jagadananda, so Mahaprabhu agreed to eat first. Jagadananda made him eat everything he had cooked. Although the food was enough for many servings, Mahaprabhu dared not refuse whatever he offered. At last he finished and asked Jagadananda to sit down and eat. But Jagadananda excused himself, saying he must first serve the others who had helped cook.

"Please go with Govinda for your massage and rest. Don't worry about me—I will eat later," he insisted. Mahaprabhu left, but he did not rest until he heard from Govinda that Jagadananda had eaten.

········

YEARS PASSED AS SRI CHAITANYA MAHAPRABHU stayed in Puri tasting transcendental love with his devotees. During the day he sang, danced, and visited Jagannath in the temple, while at night, with his close friends such as Svarup Damodar and Ramananda Raya, he listened to poems and songs describing Krishna, the beautiful cowherd boy of Vrindavan. Increasingly, at these times he felt deep and uncontrollable emotions and his moods became more and more unpredictable.

Haridas was now an elderly man. Each day Govinda brought him sacred food from Jagannath's offering. One day, Govinda found him lying on his back, hardly able to chant Krishna's names. With great effort, Haridas took a small portion of Jagannath's *prasadam*. Afterward, he said that, since he had been unable to finish chanting his fixed number of holy names on the previous day, he would fast. Govinda hurried back to Mahaprabhu and reported that Haridas was very weak.

The following day Mahaprabhu came to visit Haridas and asked him how he was.

"My body is well, but my mind is disturbed, for I cannot complete my chanting."

"Now that you are old you can reduce your daily chanting," Mahaprabhu assured him. "You have already achieved all you were sent into this world to do, for you have taught everyone the glories of Krishna's name." But Haridas made a special plea.

"I am the lowest of men, and you rescued me and allowed me to be your servant. You have made me dance in many ways. Now, my master, I have one remaining desire. I foresee that soon you will leave this world. I do not wish to see that closing chapter of this glorious story. Before this comes, let me leave this life in your presence, gazing into your moonlike face, with your lotus feet upon my heart while I chant your name."

"My dear Haridas, if this is your desire then surely Krishna will fulfill it. But how can I continue to live if you go from here and leave me?"

"I am insignificant among your dazzling associates. If an ant dies, what is the loss?" responded Haridas.

Mahaprabhu embraced him and promised to return the next day. The following morning, he brought with him all his dearmost devotees. They surrounded Haridas.

"What is the news, Haridas?" inquired Sri Chaitanya Mahaprabhu.

"Whatever mercy you can give me, my Lord," Haridas whispered.

With this, Mahaprabhu began chanting. The devotees joined him, encircling Haridas and singing with great earnestness. As they uttered the holy name, Mahaprabhu recounted the life of Haridas Thakur, the great teacher of *kirtan*. While he spoke, Haridas grasped his feet and held them to his chest. He fixed his eyes upon Mahaprabhu's shining face and chanted Krishna's names with renewed strength, tears coursing down his cheeks. As he chanted, he gave up his life in front of everyone.

Their chanting increased in intensity while Mahaprabhu raised Haridas's body, which weighed almost nothing, and danced with it down to the sea. There they bathed the body and, with due ceremony, interred it in a grave near the shore, digging in the sand with their bare hands. In the grave they placed sacred remnants from Jagannath, and Mahaprabhu threw sand onto Haridas's body. They made a platform over the place and protected it with fencing. Then they danced and chanted around it in ecstasy. After they all bathed in the sea, Mahaprabhu led them in observing a festival in the town. He collected from the shopkeepers the ingredients for a great feast, which he personally served to everyone. Then he announced a benediction: "Whoever has witnessed this festival of the passing of Haridas Thakur will soon achieve Krishna. Such is the power of seeing Haridas. Krishna was merciful to me and gave me his company. Now, being independent, Krishna has broken that companionship. Haridas left by his own will and I had no power to keep him. Without him this world has lost a great jewel." Saying farewell to the devotees, Mahaprabhu left to rest, his heart filled with both joy and sorrow.

The Engulfing Ocean of Love

One day, Mahaprabhu dreamt of Krishna dancing with the forest cowherd girls, the *gopis*. Krishna played his flute, his stance artfully curved, dressed in yellow and garlanded with forest flowers. He danced with Radha in the midst of a circle of *gopis*. Seeing this wonderful vision, Mahaprabhu felt he was at last in Vrindavan.

When Govinda woke him, Mahaprabhu realized he had only been dreaming. Devastated, he sat alone on the ground, tracing patterns on the sand with his nails.

"I found Krishna, the Lord of Vrindavan, but I have lost him again," he cried, blinded by tears. "Who has taken my Krishna? Where is Vrindavan, and what is this place I have come to?"

Unable to recover his peace of mind, he spent the rest of the day mechanically going through his routine—bathing, visiting the temple, and eating. Only when evening came could he reveal his state of confusion to his confidential friends Ramananda Raya and Svarup Damodar.

"My mind has left me and gone to Vrindavan as a beggar, taking my senses as his disciples. He wears a fabulous earring—the ring of Krishna's Rasa dance with the *gopis*—and his alms bowl is carved from my hopes. His body, smeared with ashes, is covered with the cloth of anxiety. He is emaciated from fasting, and his only words are, 'Alas, Krishna!' He wanders through the forest of Vrindavan eating herbs and roots, which are the sweet remnants left behind by the *gopis* from their play with Krishna. At night he sits awake, hoping to see Krishna dancing, but is unable to find him. Thus, my mind has deserted me and I am left in a trance."

His friends tried to calm him by singing verses from *Gita Govinda* and other Vaishnava poems. Late that night, they persuaded him to lie down in his room and they went to their beds. Outside his door slept Govinda, with all three locks bolted so that he would not wander out during the night.

Mahaprabhu lay in his room chanting Krishna's names and unable to sleep. In the dead of night, Svarup awoke and heard that all was quiet. He went to look in on Mahaprabhu, but found the room empty. He could not understand how this was possible, because all the doors remained locked. He woke the others and they searched through the darkened streets of Puri, fearing for Mahaprabhu's safety. At last they found him, lying in the road near the main gate to Jagannath's temple.

With relief they gathered around, but when they saw his condition their fears increased. He was unconscious, his skin cool to the touch, and he did not appear to be breathing. Furthermore, his body was strangely elongated, his limbs distended at the joints.

Not daring to handle him, the devotees simply began chanting loudly. All at once Mahaprabhu's eyes opened and his body seemed to contract to its normal form. He sat up and recognized Svarup bending over him.

"Where am I? How did I come here?" he asked.

"Let us take you home and I will tell you everything," urged Svarup, gently. Dazed, Mahaprabhu allowed himself to be helped to his room, where Svarup told him all that had happened.

"I remember nothing of this" was his response. "All I know is that I saw Krishna, for an instant only, and then he was gone. He appeared and disappeared like a flash of lightning."

Mahaprabhu spent his days drifting in and out of external awareness. He was sometimes able to carry on his normal activities, but the least stimulus could trigger a sudden change in him. Once, when he went to the temple to see Jagannath, he was transfixed with the realization that Jagannath was Krishna himself. He heard Krishna's playful words and the sound of Krishna's flute; he felt the cool touch of Krishna's body; he smelled the musk that Krishna always wore; and he tasted the sweetness of Krishna's lips. All these sensations fought for his attention at once. Unable to steady himself, he fainted and had to be helped home. That night he tried to explain his experiences to Svarup and Ramananda.

"My mind is like a horse ridden by five riders. It cannot resist Krishna's beauty, the sound of his voice, his touch, his fragrance, or the taste of his lips. Each of my senses pulls in a different direction. All at once my mind is lost and I feel in danger of dying." Clinging to the necks of his two friends, he begged them, "What shall I do? Where shall I go? Please tell me how I shall find Krishna."

One day, walking on the beach, he saw a beautiful garden and mistook it for Vrindavan forest. Running into the garden he searched for Krishna, in the same way the *gopis* had searched in the forest after Krishna disappeared from their Rasa dance. Absorbed in the mood of the *gopis*, he spoke to the trees and creepers.

"Have you seen Krishna? Did he pass this way?" As he wandered here and there, he recited verses from the songs of the *gopis* in the forest. Ecstasies of anxiety, humility, anger, and impatience shook his body, like elephants fighting in a sugarcane field. Tossed this way and that, he suddenly saw Krishna in front of him, standing beneath a *kadamba* tree and playing the flute. He fell unconscious to the ground. His friends came and took him on their laps. Chanting to him and massaging his feet, they brought him to external awareness.

"Where has Krishna gone? I saw him, but now I have lost him," he cried when he opened his eyes. Svarup comforted him with verses from his favorite poems about Krishna, and they brought him home.

········

ON A FULL MOON NIGHT, Mahaprabhu walked with his friends along the seashore. Many times they had visited here over the years. But this night was the full moon of the autumn season, when Krishna danced all night with the *gopis* in Vrindavan. As he walked through the gardens along the shore, Mahaprabhu was lost in thoughts of Vrindavan. Different ecstatic emotions took hold of him, and he was alternately stunned, trembling, perspiring, turning pale, and weeping. Sometimes he laughed with joy, and other times he cried; sometimes he danced and sang, or he could be found running here and there; and sometimes he simply fell unconscious in the sand.

By his side walked Svarup, singing of Krishna. He sang a verse that described how after the Rasa dance Krishna and the *gopis* bathed in the waters of the Yamuna River. At that moment, Mahaprabhu saw the waves of the ocean reflecting the light of the full moon.

Unnoticed by anyone, moving with the speed of mind, he dove headlong into the waves, seeing them as the Yamuna River. He fell unconscious into the sea and floated away in the darkness before anyone had missed him. The ocean currents carried him northward along the coast, far from Puri. Under the moonlight he drifted silently through the waves, deep in trance.

As soon as his disappearance was noticed, anxiety swept his friends. Some hurried toward the temple, and others searched the town; some looked in the seafront gardens, and others went as far as the Gundicha temple. Eventually, all of them returned to the beach. Their hopes of finding Mahaprabhu began to fade; they imagined a disaster had taken place and they would never see him again.

As they searched the seashore in the darkness, a fisherman ran toward them. He was laughing, crying, dancing, and repeatedly singing the name "Hari!" But when they spoke to him, he was full of fear.

"Why are you acting like this? What have you seen?" they asked.

"I caught a dead body in my net," replied the fisherman. "At first, I thought it was a big fish, but when I saw it was a body I tried to release it back into the water. Accidentally, I touched it and now a ghost has entered me, making me mad. I can't stop shivering and crying."

"Tell us more. What did this body look like?"

"It was very long, with extended limbs loosened at the joints. Sometimes I fancied it opened its eyes and made a murmuring sound. I am frightened to go back there."

Svarup persuaded him to lead them to the place where he had left the body. There they found Mahaprabhu in a desperate condition, his body bleached white by the sea and covered in sand. Carefully they wiped him clean and laid him on a fresh cloth. Then they chanted loudly. For a long time they continued to sing and nothing happened. Then Mahaprabhu stirred and got up. His body seemed fully recovered, but he was not aware of his surroundings.

"I went to Vrindavan and saw the River Yamuna," he said, hardly seeing his companions. "There I watched Krishna sporting with the *gopis* in the water. The *gopis* dressed in white were like lightning, and Krishna was dark like a rain cloud. They showered water upon each other, fighting hand to hand, then face to face, chest to chest, teeth to teeth, and finally nail to nail. There seemed to be thousands of *gopis* and thousands of Krishnas. Radha was there and Krishna captured her. He took her into the deep water, where she clung to his neck to save herself and floated like a lotus flower. Then Krishna quarrelled with her and the *gopis* closed around to give her protection. They looked like a cluster of white lotus flowers.

"When this play was over, the *gopis* arranged a picnic on the riverbank, where a small jeweled house stood among the trees and creepers. They served Krishna many kinds of fruits and sweets cooked by Radharani. When he had eaten, and Radha and the *gopis* had tasted his remnants, he lay down with Radha in the jeweled house, fanned by the *gopis*. Then everyone fell asleep. I saw all this and my mind was at peace until all of a sudden you made a great noise and brought me back here. Now I have lost Vrindavan and the Yamuna, and I don't know where Krishna and the *gopis* have gone."

Svarup consoled Mahaprabhu and told him how, while he was in ecstasy, they had been in agony, searching for him all night. Submissively, he allowed them to help him bathe in the sea and then to take him home.

Day and Night

Each year, Jagadananda used to travel to Navadvip to visit Mahaprabhu's mother with news and gifts from her son. Many years had passed since mother and son had met, when one year he sent her a poignant message.

"Mother, when I gave up your service to become a *sannyasi,* I broke my religious principles, and because of this I have become mad. You told me to stay here in Jagannath Puri, and here I must stay to the end of my life. Please forgive me, for I depend on you always."

When Advaita Acharya heard of this message, he gave Jagadananda a message of his own to take back to Mahaprabhu. It contained a mysterious poem. Jagadananda memorized the poem and on his return recited it.

"Tell Sri Chaitanya Mahaprabhu we have all become mad like him. Say there is no more demand for rice in the marketplace. Say that all of us who are mad have lost interest in the material world. This message comes from one who has also become mad."

Mahaprabhu smiled at these words, saying, "This is Advaita's order to me."

Svarup asked him the meaning of the poem.

"Advaita Acharya is expert in the art of worship. He invites the deity to come and receive worship. Then, when the worship is complete, and there is no more need, he sends the deity away. His words are full of meaning, for he is a great mystic."

As he pondered Advaita's message, Mahaprabhu's thoughts turned to Krishna's leaving Vrindavan. The *gopis* had surrounded his chariot and pleaded with him to stay, but Krishna had left. Radha then spoke to her friend Vishakha and her despairing words were recorded in the *Bhagavatam*. Mahaprabhu now spoke these same words, clinging to Ramananda and speaking to Svarup as if he were a *gopi*.

"My dear friend, where is Krishna, who rises like the moon from the ocean of Nanda Maharaja? Where is Krishna, whose head is decorated with a peacock feather? Where is Krishna, whose flute vibrates such a deep sound, and who is so expert in dancing the Rasa dance? He is the only one who can save my life. Please tell me where I can find Krishna! My heart breaks at not seeing his face. Show him to me now, or else I will die. Providence, you are so cruel! First you reveal Krishna's beautiful face and captivate my eyes; then after a moment, you take him away."

Svarup and Ramananda did their best to calm him. They sang to him of the *gopis* meeting Krishna and enjoying his company. Soothed by these thoughts, but still unhappy, he was persuaded to lie down for the night, with Svarup and Govinda sleeping outside his door to safeguard him. During the night, he continued to chant, and thoughts of separation from Krishna drove him wild. He tried to leave the room but could not, because they had bolted the doors. He threw himself against the walls, bruising his tender face and body. Svarup, awakened by his cries of distress, lit a lamp and went in to see him. When he saw the bruises on his body, his face scratched and tearful, Svarup felt deep sorrow.

"What have you done to yourself?" he said, soothing him and taking him back to his bed. At such times, Svarup remembered a verse from the poem *Krishna-Karnamrita*, often recited by Mahaprabhu: "Because I have not met you, my days and nights have become unbearable. They are not passing and it is difficult for me to know how to live through all this time. Kindly give me your audience, for I am in a precarious position."

In this and many ways, from that day when he received Advaita's message, Sri Chaitanya Mahaprabhu's ecstasies deepened. He became inconsolable in his feelings of separation from Krishna. Day and night he could not rest, tossed on the waves of the endless ocean of love for God.

·······

IN BETWEEN HIS DRAWN-OUT ECSTASIES, in the lucid moments that Svarup called external consciousness, Mahaprabhu confided to his two companions his deep spiritual convictions. Earlier in his life, he had composed eight verses to guide people on the spiritual path. Now he repeated them, elaborating on their deep meaning.

"My friends, chanting God's names is the best spiritual path in this Age of Kali. Hear me when I say:

> "Glory be to our chanting of Krishna's name, which washes the dust of years from the mirror of the heart, extinguishes the blazing fire of birth and death, spreads the shining moon of good fortune, and inspires true wisdom. This chanting expands the ocean of bliss, and gives all who bathe in that ocean a taste of the sweetest nectar at every step."

"Chanting awakens my desire to serve Krishna," he continued. "Through chanting I achieve Krishna's company and the opportunity to serve him. This service is like an ocean of nectar." In humility and gratitude, he felt he had no love for Krishna's holy name, so he recited his second verse:

> "O my Lord, your many names contain all your personal potencies, and there are no rules for how or when to chant them. Your mercy is so great, yet my misfortune is that I have no attraction for your names."

"Because different people desire different things," he explained, "the Lord has given many different names for us to chant. Regardless of time or place, we can chant in any way, and so achieve all perfection. Now I will tell you the best way to chant:

> "One who feels lower than the grass, who is more tolerant than a tree, who expects no personal honor, but who gives all honor to others, can easily chant the name of the Lord constantly."

"If a tree is mistreated it still gives fruit and shelter without protesting or even asking for water. So a humble Vaishnava, who knows that Krishna lives in all beings, respects them all and asks them for nothing. If you chant in this mood, you will certainly awaken your love for God." As he spoke, his humility grew and he prayed for the gift of service:

"O Supreme Lord! I have no desire to enjoy wealth, fame, or a beautiful partner. All I want, birth after birth, is to offer you pure devotional service.

"O Krishna, I am your eternal servant, but I have fallen into this ocean of birth and death. Please be merciful and accept me as a particle of dust at your lotus feet."

Saying these prayers, he felt the deep desire to chant Krishna's name in ecstatic love, and continued:

"When will tears stream from my eyes, words falter in my throat, and my hairs stand on end, by chanting your name?"

Overcome with feelings of separation from Krishna, he began to lose his peace of mind. In distress, he recited his seventh verse:

"A moment seems like a thousand years, tears flow from my eyes like torrents of rain, all the world appears vacant—without you, Govinda."

He remembered Radha's words: "A day never ends, my eyes are like clouds in the monsoon, I am burning in a slow fire, Krishna ignores me to test my love. My friends say I should forget him, but I cannot." Absorbed in Radharani's mood he spoke his heart:

"Let Krishna embrace me as I fall at his feet, or trample me beneath him, or let him even break my heart by leaving me. He is free to do anything and everything, for he will always be the unconditional Lord of my heart."

Speaking like this, he was overwhelmed by Radha's ecstasies of pure love for Krishna. He entered deeper and deeper into her conflicting emotions and his mind became unsteady. So he passed his time like a mad person in the company of his two friends, while they consoled him with songs of love for Krishna.

········

As a *sannyasi*, he had traveled and preached for six years. In Jagannath Puri for a further six years, he shared his love for God with his followers by chanting the Hare Krishna mantra. For the last twelve years of his life, he experienced separation from Krishna day and night, crying and talking in ecstasy. After twelve years of this constant rapture of love, he could no longer sustain his body and mind. In 1534, at the age of forty-eight, he left this world. Some say he was carried out to sea; others, that he merged with the deity of Jagannath, or with Tota Gopinath, worshipped in Puri by his dearest friend, Gadadhar. Whatever the truth, he left no earthly remains.

Sri Chaitanya Mahaprabhu left behind a network of pure devotees of Krishna through whom his memory and teachings lived on, and he left his eight verses called *Sikshastaka*, cited above. These verses are the jewel of all Vaishnava literature, for they enshrine the highest truths of spiritual life and embody all that he lived and taught. Wherever his words are remembered and his name is sung, he lives on.

This was his promise.

"You, my dear devotees, are with me birth after birth. I will never leave you, even for a moment."

ENDNOTES

1. *Viraha-bhakti*, or "love in separation," is a main tenet of Chaitanya Vaishnavism. It is related to the principle of "separation makes the heart grow fonder." Vaishnava teachers have written extensively about divine union (*sambhoga*) and how it is enhanced by feelings of distance and longing.

2. Nityananda was not related to Chaitanya, but the two felt an intimate connection as brothers. According to tradition, Chaitanya was Krishna and Nityananda was an incarnation of Balaram, Krishna's brother, making them brothers in a spiritual sense.

3. Although Advaita means "not two," implying the truth that all is one, he taught that service requires two: the one serving and the one being served.

4. Gadadhar is viewed as an incarnation of Krishna's *shakti*, his internal energy.

5. Srivas is viewed as an incarnation of the sage Narada, whose stories are told throughout the Puranas. He is the messenger of Krishna who lives to spread the holy name from universe to universe.

6. The Goddess here refers to Durga, the Divine Mother, who fulfills the wishes of her children living in the earthly realm.

7. Krishna as a child used to steal food and break pots in the village of Vraja. Therefore, the ladies of Navadvip, identifying child Nimai with Krishna, were thrilled when he reminded them of him.

8. Lakshmipriya is revered as an incarnation of Lakshmi, the Goddess of Fortune.

9. The standard biographies state that Lakshmipriya passed away from "the snake bite of separation," implying that the external reason for her death may have been an actual snakebite, while the spiritual reason was her longing for Nimai.

10. In those days it was not uncommon for a traveling mendicant to stay at a person's home to bless them with knowledge. In reciprocation, the householder would fulfill any request the mendicant might have. While asking for one's son as a traveling companion was uncommon, it was not unheard of. Some *brahmana* families considered it an honor, and expected their child to be trained in spiritual life under a wandering ascetic.

11. This saying illustrates the Vaishnava understanding of Nityananda as the original guru. According to Vaishnava teaching, one approaches Krishna through the guru, i.e., one first gives respect to the guru and then to Krishna.

12. According to the *Chaitanya-bhagavata* (Madhya 20.58), Vishvambhar actually showed Haridas his own back at this point, and Haridas saw the scars that should have been on his own back.

13. At that time in India, the life of a *sannyasa* (renunciant) was widely respected, and although it would have been a tremendous sacrifice for Chaitanya to become one, he was willing to do it for his *sankirtan* movement. Life as a *sannyasi* is often difficult—begging from door to door and living in austere conditions, constantly traveling. Chaitanya's loved ones could not bear the thought of his living a hard life, nor did they want to live without his association.

14. Chaitanya wanted to be initiated by Keshava Bharati in the lineage of Shankara because part of Chaitanya's mission was to convince Mayavadi philosophers of personalism, and they would more easily listen to a *sannyasi* in their own tradition. Interestingly, Keshava Bharati is viewed as an incarnation of Akrura, who in Krishna-lila took Krishna out of Vrindavan, causing the *gopis* and his other loving associates who lived there to experience love in separation. In a similar way, Keshava Bharati, by initiating Chaitanya as a *sannyasi,* helped him leave Navadvip, causing his friends and family to experience a similar sense of love in separation.

15. Normally, a man does not take *sannyasa* until he is in his fifties. Vishvambhar was only twenty-four years old, but his determination was exceptional, virtually forcing Keshava Bharati to initiate him.

16. There is a reason that Nityananda broke the staff. Since Chaitanya took *sannyasa* in a Shankarite lineage, he would have carried an *ekadanda* (single staff), symbolizing his oneness with God. However, as a Vaishnava, he would be more inclined to carrying a *tridanda* (triple staff), as Vaishnava *sannyasis* do, for this indicates surrendering "mind, body, and words" in the service of God.

17. The devotees actually conspired to help Prataparudra meet Chaitanya. At first, Ramananda Raya interceded on the King's behalf, seeing if Chaitanya would at least agree to meet the King's son. After all, he said, "a son is one's own self born again." The devotees thus brought the boy into Chaitanya's association.

The King's son was dark-hued and looked like Krishna, and so Chaitanya was immediately drawn to him. When he saw the boy, in fact, he embraced him, making the young prince swoon with ecstatic love for Krishna. Later, the boy went to his father, Prataparudra, who naturally hugged his son. Like an electrical circuit, the love poured from Chaitanya through the son to Prataparudra himself.

Feeling the ecstasy of Chaitanya's association, even indirectly like this, the King wanted to be in his presence more than ever. Consequently, Sarvabhauma devised a plan: at the Rathayatra festival, Chaitanya would naturally dance like a divine madman (*divya-mada*) before the cart of Jagannath. Afterward, he would want to rest, and would lie down in a nearby garden. At that point, the King could, in the dress of a commoner, approach Chaitanya and gain his association. It is this part of the story that is told here.

18. Significantly, when Nityananda returned to Bengal, he married. Varuni and Revati were the wives of Balaram in the spiritual world; they manifested in Caitanya's world as Vasudha and Jahnava. After Nityananda's demise, Jahnava became a leading figure in the Gaudiya Vaishnava lineage.

19. In the time elapsing since Chaitanya and Tapan Mishra first met in East Bengal, the latter had a son, Raghunath Bhatta Goswami, one of the Six Goswamis of Vrindavan, who became a teacher in Varanasi.

INDEX

Following pages: *Chaitanya's message was embodied in the five people united in a single love. They were, left to right, Advaita, Nityananda, Chaitanya, Gadadhara and Shrivas; together they are the five truths of devotion: Pancha Tattva.*

···· ꧁꧂ ····

ACKNOWLEDGMENTS

········

The idea for this book came from my publisher Ramdas (Raoul Goff). I was doubtful I could do it, but he never was. I immersed myself in the literature of Sri Chaitanya and found new inspiration from the sixteenth-century writings of Krishna Das, translated and commented on by my teacher A.C. Bhaktivedanta Swami Prabhupada; and from the works of Vrindavan Das, transparently and poetically translated by my godbrother Kusakratha Das. During this book's long gestation, I stayed for some time with my godbrother Kesava Bharati Dasa Goswami in Govardhan. He gave me boundless support and encouragement. ❧ Our intention was for the great Indian artists B. G. Sharma to produce a unique set of paintings to illustrate this book. I spent several weeks with him at his home in Udaipur, helping him prepare preliminary sketches. However, providence took him away from this world before he could progress further. Thereafter an extraordinary set of unattributed paintings of the life of Sri Chaitanya came to light in Bengal. It was common until the early twentieth century for devotee artists in India, in a spirit of non-ego, not to sign their work. Hence, we are unable to trace the name of the artist. However, the paintings can now receive the appreciation they richly deserve. ❧ Janardana Das (Jan Brzezinski) advised on my first draft, and after a long delay, my dear friend Yogesvara Das (Joshua Greene) agreed to be my editor. He injected new energy into the project and persuaded me to extensively revise what I had thought was my final draft. I am glad he did—the book is the better for it. He was assisted by Jan Hughes, Jane Chinn, and Binh Matthews at Insight Editions and Mandala Publishing, under the energetic guidance of Ramdas. I am grateful to them all. ❧ Writing a book is always a longer journey than expected. This book, taking me into new realms of experience, took ten years to realise. I hope my publisher and readers will find it worth the wait.

COLOPHON

·······

Publisher: Raoul Goff
Art Director: Chrissy Kwasnik
Designer: Dagmar Trojanek
Editor: Joshua Greene
Associate Managing Editor: Jan Hughes
Production Manager: Jane Chinn

INSIGHT EDITIONS would like to thank Judith Dunham and Ken Dellapenta.